The Birth of Jazz

The Birth of Jazz

Reviving the Music of the Bolden Era

Daniel Hardie

iUniverse, Inc.
New York Lincoln Shanghai

The Birth of Jazz
Reviving the Music of the Bolden Era

Copyright © 2007 by Daniel Hardie

All rights reserved. No part of this book may be used or reproduced by any means, graphic, electronic, or mechanical, including photocopying, recording, taping or by any information storage retrieval system without the written permission of the publisher except in the case of brief quotations embodied in critical articles and reviews.

iUniverse books may be ordered through booksellers or by contacting:

iUniverse
2021 Pine Lake Road, Suite 100
Lincoln, NE 68512
www.iuniverse.com
1-800-Authors (1-800-288-4677)

The views expressed in this work are solely those of the author and do not necessarily reflect the views of the publisher, and the publisher hereby disclaims any responsibility for them.

ISBN-13: 978-0-595-42555-6 (pbk)
ISBN-13: 978-0-595-86884-1 (ebk)
ISBN-10: 0-595-42555-0 (pbk)
ISBN-10: 0-595-86884-3 (ebk)

Printed in the United States of America

For Tracey and Melissa

"I talked of constructing an illusion of the unattainable past, and that is not what they wished to hear."

—Norman Davies[1]

---

1   Davies Norman "Europe East and West"

Contents

List of Illustrations xi

Introduction xiii

Chapter 1. New Orleans and the Birth of Jazz 1

Chapter 2. The Social Dance Evening 11

Chapter 3. The Creators of Jazz 25

Chapter 4. The Repertoire Part 1
               Popular Songs and Rags 36

Chapter 5. The Repertoire Part 2
               Black Vernacular Songs and Blues 51

Chapter 6. How They Played 66

Chapter 7. Reconstructing Elemental Jazz 76

Chapter 8. Not Quite Ragtime 84

Chapter 9. Historically Informed Performance 96

Chapter 10. The Heritage of Elemental Jazz 107

Chapter 11. Revivals in Retrospect 121

Bibliography 133

Appendix 1. Jelly Roll Morton's demonstration of *La Praline Quadrille* 139

Appendix 2. A Guide to the Performance of Early Jazz 143

About the Author 163

Index 165

List of Illustrations

Fig.1 Canal St. New Orleans 2

Fig.2 The Port of New Orleans 3

Fig.3 Economy Hall 12

Fig.4 The Artisan (Artesian) Hall 13

Fig.5 Social Dancin' 14

Fig.6 The Funky Butt Hall 17

Fig.7 New Orleans Street band 27

Fig.8 Buddy Bolden, Jefferson Mumford, Manuel Perez and Jimmy Brown 29

Fig.9 Joe Petit and Jimmy Johnson 31

Fig.10 Any Rags 41

Fig.11 Shoo Skeeter Shoo 42

Fig.12 Wait till the Sun Shines Nellie 44

Fig.13 Vernacular dancin' 52

Fig.14 Go Down Moses 62

Fig.15 Will Cornish and Willie Warner 67

Fig.16 The Buddy Bolden Revival Orchestra 82

Fig.17 Jack Carey and Kid Ory 115

Fig.18 The Original Creole Orchestra 116

Table 1 The Revised Bolden Repertoire 37

Chart 1 The First Generation of Jazz Bands 32
Chart 2 Passing on the Heritage 119
Ex.1 Ragging the Tune 74
Cover Photo: Buddy Bolden's Orchestra ca1905

Introduction

"The word is believed to derive from *jasi* which in the language of the Mandingo tribe of West Africa means 'to act out of the ordinary'".

—Mary Cable[2]

It is a strange thing that, though most books about the history of jazz allude briefly to its birth, they appear to be incurious about the actual circumstances.

Most mention, if only briefly, the music of Buddy Bolden and though they may include references to a number of his successors, they devote very little attention to the first ten years of the life of jazz, and many begin with the Northern career of the first recorded jazz band, starting in 1917, some twenty years after its beginning.

Bolden's story has been very well told by his biographer Donald M. Marquis[3], and in my own *The Loudest Trumpet—Buddy Bolden and the Early History of Jazz* I sought to detail some of the musical features of his career and relate them to the later history of jazz.[4]

In my second work *"Exploring Early Jazz—The Origins and Evolution of the New Orleans Style"* I presented a chronological account of what had been documented of the first thirty years of jazz as it developed into the hot music of the Jazz Age, beginning with Elemental Jazz of Bolden and his contemporaries.[5]

My research into this early period threw up many questions as to its roots that led to my work on its musical origins—*"The Ancestry of Jazz–*

---

2   Cable Mary "Lost New Orleans" 1980
3   Marquis D. "In Search of Buddy Bolden" 1978/93
4   Hardie D. "The Loudest Trumpet—Buddy Bolden and the Early History of Jazz" 2000
5   Hardie D. "Exploring Early Jazz—The Origins and Evolution of the New Orleans Style" 2002

A Musical Family History". This, in its turn, led me to enquire more fully into the nature of the music itself and its initial appearance and form.[6]

Since 2004 I have been collecting original musical material and applying what is known about the earliest jazz in order to demonstrate, in performance, its character and range.

As early as 1958 jazz historian Sam Charters published a compendium of details about early New Orleans jazz music and musicians.[7] Unfortunately though it contained a vast amount of information, and many colourful accounts of their performances, little attention was paid to listing the source of such accounts, though with a little attention to the detail, it is possible to match some accounts with information supplied by witnesses in the oral history archives, or from other written sources.

He wrote for example:

> "Bolden was the colourful personality, and when his band 'improvised' a "blues" in public at a dance in Globe Hall in the summer of 1894 or 1895 he became famous as the man ...'who invented the hot blues'."

This piece of information, alone, if it could be verified, might be considered to give us a precise date for our consideration of jazz beginnings. There were, indeed, other witnesses who confirmed the widely held suggestion that Bolden was the first to introduce the blues to dancing, and we know he played at the Globe Hall in St. Peter St. However Charters did not provide any support for his imprecise dating. Marquis established that Bolden began learning the cornet in 1894 (when he was about 17), and he apparently learned quite quickly to participate in local dance music.

There is other evidence suggesting that some of the elements of what we consider jazz performance style were derived from much earlier musical sources and may have started to influence New Orleans music around the same time.

There is also considerable confusion about the interpretation of terms like rag and ragtime in the context of New Orleans music around the second decade of the 1890's, and although the term jazz may have appeared earlier in the city and elsewhere, it was not applied to New Orleans style dance music before 1916.[8]

---

6   Hardie D. "The Ancestry of Jazz—A Musical Family History" 2004
7   Charters S. "New Orleans Jazz 1895/1963" 1958/63
8   see Gushee L."Pioneers of Jazz The Story of the Creole Band" 2005 pp 299-302

Be that as it may, in the last five years of the 19th Century significant changes began to appear in the performance of dance music in the city though, as we shall see, the style and content of the social dance evening itself does not seem to have changed much.

Unfortunately, as I have pointed out elsewhere, the paucity of resources of annotated information about the development of white jazz music before 1910 limits our ability to compare it with what other sources tell us about early black bands. I suspect that the interconnections between the two groups, separated though they were by social barriers, began quite early.

All of the above suggests that we need to examine in some detail the processes by which the jazz revolution came about at that time, along with the musical environment, social and historical factors, popular culture and personal and family influences involved. There were, for example, Creole families with an established tradition of professional dance band performance who successfully made the transition to the new style and probably contributed to shaping its early development. We may even be able to identify how some of the new styles of instrumental performance emerged from the old.

In previous works dealing with early jazz I have sometimes found it necessary to repeat, for the convenience of readers of the later books, material from the earlier ones. So too, with this one, which deals with the beginnings of jazz it will be necessary to amplify and develop to some degree material found in the later chapters of *"The Ancestry of Jazz—A Musical Family History"*. The emphasis in this work will not be on new research. Rather I propose to focus on the events surrounding the birth of jazz in order to bring to life the music, its audience and its creators.

I propose also to incorporate, where necessary, new research material that has been published or reappeared since my researches began in the late 1990's. A good example of this is Professor Lawrence Gushee's detailed account of the history of the Original Creole Orchestra[9]. New information has also become available about the origins of the Bolden family and the disputed birth date of Bunk Johnson, one of the significant witnesses to the birth of jazz.

D. Hardie 2006

---

9   Gushee L. op cit 2005

Chapter 1

New Orleans and the Birth of Jazz

"One thing is certain, New Orleans Jazz began in New Orleans"

—L. Gushee

There is no birth certificate that records the birth of jazz, nor even a notice in the local press. Such documents, if properly compiled, would announce the date of the event, where it took place, the name given to the offspring, parentage and even possibly nominate witnesses to the event. They would also grant a degree of legitimacy sadly lacking in the story of jazz. Since at least the 1940's jazz historians have squabbled about its origins, its nature and even its name.[10]

In a previous work I adopted a very simple dictionary definition of jazz that appears to encompass the features of the music I am talking about[11] and I have also limited my discourse to the New Orleans Style, a musical form that most authorities agree appeared around the end of the 19th Century.

The Music of New Orleans

New Orleans began life as a French colony in 1699 and, although for a long period after 1763 it was ruled by Spain, its music began and

---

10   See Hardie D. "Exploring Early Jazz-The Origins and Evolution of the New Orleans Style" 2002 p11 and Gushee L. "Pioneers of Jazz—The Story of the Creole Band" 2005 pp 299/302
11   "Syncopated dance music that is wholly or partly improvised"

remained dominated by French trained musicians until the coming of the Americans in 1803, when the United States purchased it from the Emperor Napoleon, who had regained the province shortly before this so-called 'Louisiana Purchase'.

During the Colonial Period the fashionable classes attended masquerade balls, state dinners and lavish parties dancing the Allemandes, Courantes, Gavottes, Gigues, Minuets and Sarabandes then popular in France.[12]

Fig.1 Above: Canal St. around 1900, the busy boundary between the Downtown French Quarter on left of picture and Uptown on right

Theatres and Opera houses were established, ballrooms were built and the Mardi Gras tradition was established. During this time a large segment of the free population were of mixed parentage and known as Creoles or *Gens de Couleur Libre*. This group largely adhered to the musical traditions of France.

Before 1803 the large African slave population, many of whom came to New Orleans from Cuba and other Spanish colonies were treated

---

[12] The material in this section is necessarily abbreviated. A fuller account of history music in New Orleans before jazz can be found in the author's "The Ancestry of Jazz—A Musical Family History" 2004 Chapter 13

with a degree of tolerance and permitted to perform their own African music, though, by 1800, there were strong Spanish and Creole influences appearing in the slave music. Slaves also began adopting European forms of dance, like jigs and reels played on European instruments. The main venue for slave performances was the so-called Congo Square.

In the years before the Civil War, New Orleans composers (white and Creole) began to appear, the best known of whom was Louis Moreau Gottschalk, who incorporated in many of his compositions elements drawn from Cuban and slave music.

With the coming of the American governors in 1803 something of a tightening in race relations began. The slave dances were eventually discontinued. Immigration from European countries brought increasing numbers of musicians trained in the European musical tradition.

Creole musicians also continued to be trained in the practices of European music. Entertainment began to be provided in local dance halls for Creole Social Clubs by "bands of music", believed to be largely string groups—using violins, cellos, mandolins, and perhaps guitars. Brass bands seem to have been active before 1861.

Fig.2 Above: The busy port and railway depot of New Orleans with upriver paddle steamers.

The Civil War[13] caused considerable disruption. New Orleans was quickly occupied by Federal troops and considerable numbers of slaves entered the city as refugees from Confederate held plantations. The Federal authorities began regular concerts performed by military bands. The 1860's also saw the emergence of rough barrelhouses and concert-saloons that catered for dancing to piano or fiddle.

With the end of the war and the freeing of the slaves the City remained under Federal government. Large numbers of former slaves migrated from plantations to the city, moving into the Uptown section that had been occupied by the Americans since 1803. This Reconstruction period lasted until 1877. During this time local dance hall entertainments, parades and picnics, flourished, featuring string orchestras and increasingly brass bands. This trend continued in the 1880's.

The last twenty years of the century saw the emergence of mixed string and wind orchestras in which some brass instruments were added to the string component. They varied in size but might comprise one or two violins, cornets, clarinet, trombone, bass violin and late in the 1890's trap drummers. They played arrangements of the songs and dances of the day, Waltzes, Quadrilles, Lancers, Schottisches and later ragtime songs.

In this period a further influx of Spanish American musicians occurred. Mexican bands, Cuban or Spanish Orquestas Typicas and itinerant Spanish musicians appeared. There was also a flourishing street music tradition.

Before the Civil War the predominant Creole population was Catholic and religious music followed the rituals of the Church. There were also a few protestant churches influenced by the Revivalist music of the 1840's. With the immigration of former slaves after 1870 came an increase in Baptist Holy Roller churches that sang Jubilees, Shouts and Spirituals which preserved elements of earlier African shout music melded with the sacred songs of the white revivalists.

This was the musical tradition into which jazz was to be born.

Why New Orleans?

What was so special about New Orleans that jazz was born there? A number of writers have tried to suggest that it was something about

---

13   1861/1865

the musical environment that led to the coming of jazz—they saw it as the offspring of a melting pot of racial musical influences. Others have suggested that its emergence there was no more than part of a national movement towards syncopated music that occurred in many places around the same time.

The melting pot theory is attractive. Jelly Roll Morton said:

> "Y'know, New Orleans was inhabited with maybe every race on the face of the globe. And of course, we had Spanish people; they had plenty of 'em. And plenty o' French people."[14]

However, in practice, it is difficult to support the idea of a musical culture in New Orleans that, before the birth of jazz, differed significantly from the common musical culture of the United States.[15]

Similarly, though the idea that jazz appeared spontaneously in cities all over the country was popular for a time, it too, is difficult to substantiate. Certainly we can point to a few musicians, like Philadelphia's black composer Francis Johnson who, before 1844, was reputed to have improvised rhythmic variations on simple melodies that transformed them into jigs or reels. However, early recordings of dance music from bands playing in other cities around 1900 do not, in general, display the same characteristics of improvisation and syncopation that appeared with the earliest recordings of New Orleans jazz bands.[16]

Scientists will usually prefer the simplest hypothesis that can explain an event or phenomenon. It seems to me that the simplest explanation of the fact that I was born in Sydney, Australia, is the genealogist's explanation: I was born here because it is where my parents were at the time. It was if you like an accident of birth.

Similarly it is tempting to conclude that New Orleans jazz was born in New Orleans because the people who created it were there. Historians will perhaps perceive in this view a variation of the 'great man theory' of history[17], and it begs the question.

---

14 Library of Congress recording Jm28
15 See Hardie D. "The Ancestry of Jazz-A Musical family History" Chapter 13 particularly p166 and pp173/177.
16 Cuban recordings ca 1906 do, however, show some similarities.
17 This much disputed theory argues that great men create history and its antithesis, that history creates great men. So either Hitler changed the course of the 20th Century or the events of the 1920's created Hitler.

Who Created Jazz?

Unfortunately the answer leads us into another of the disputed regions of jazz history and criticism.

The **'white origins theory'** has two strands.

In 1917 the Chicago based New Orleans band called The Original Dixieland Jass Band (Original Dixieland Five) made the first jazz recordings. This coincided with the earliest use of the term 'jass' or jazz to describe syncopated music.

The recordings were immediately successful and they created a worldwide interest in the music and the word jazz was quickly adopted. Bands everywhere copied the 'new' style.

The leader of the Original Dixieland Jazz Band (ODJB) was cornetist Nick La Rocca. La Rocca maintained for the rest of his life that they invented jazz in Chicago and that there was nothing like it in New Orleans. This priority, and even the first use of the word jazz, was hotly disputed by two other white New Orleans band leaders; Johnny Stein, an earlier leader of the group that subsequently became known as the ODJB[18], and Tom Brown who led his 'Band from Dixieland', was in Chicago around the same time. Brown a dedicated segregationist also maintained that jazz owed nothing to the influence of black New Orleans musicians.[19]

A second 'white origins theory' takes us back to the mid 1890's. This account relies on the appearance of a group of white boy street singers who started performing around 1896—The Razzy Dazzy Spasm Band. The leader, known as "Stale bread" (Emile Lacoume), claimed to be the inventor of jazz. Subsequently a group of white musicians are said to have copied the style turning it into an instrumental form. (Possibly Johnny Stein's group that then included clarinettist Alcide Nunez)[20]

White brass band leader Jack Laine also claimed to have had bands that ragged the tunes in the 1890's and he is considered by many to have been the father of white jazz. Laine, too, was reluctant to admit

---

18 Billed in Chicago as "Stein's Original Dixieland Jazz Band"
19 This story is detailed in Hardie D. "Exploring Early Jazz—the Origins and Evolution of the New Orleans Style" 2002 p187ff
20 Also detailed in Hardie D. "Exploring Early Jazz—the Origins and Evolution of the New Orleans Style" 2002 p171ff

any influence from black music, though in one interview he said he had heard Buddy Bolden.[21]

La Rocca's claim to have invented jazz in 1917 has had some adherents, but in general it has had little critical support, and a number of his contemporaries stated that they were influenced by black music they heard in New Orleans. While it seems possible that jazz acquired influences from white sources detailed information has not come forward about white bands before around 1910, and this is much too late. The contribution of white musicians to early jazz therefore remains an open question.

The most widely accepted theory of the origins of jazz is that it originated in New Orleans, notably in the Buddy Bolden Orchestra of 1896/1906, and later spread to Chicago and other points North. Recent data suggests that it began to spread North and East around 1905 and became widely known on the vaudeville stage promoted by the extensive circuit tours of The Original Creole Orchestra between 1914 and 1917, before coming to international attention with the ODJB recordings of 1917.

Fortunately this **"Black origins" theory** is well supported by oral testimony of contemporary witnesses[22] and biographical research. This data also enables us to flesh out details of the beginnings. If Buddy Bolden did not himself invent the music we now call jazz many of his contemporaries believed it first appeared in his performances before 1900.

In a previous work I decided to divide my consideration of early jazz history into three overlapping decades: The first generation of bands (1896/1907) ending with the end of Bolden's career in 1906 or 1907. The second decade concluded with the recordings of the ODJB in 1917 and the third including the music of the Jazz Age and Classic Jazz (1917/1927).[23] This work will concentrate and focus on the circumstances of the birth of jazz and its first ten years.

---

21 Marquis D. op cit p 34 footnote 13
22 Many of the records of interviews are held in the Hogan Jazz Archive at Tulane University (New Orleans). References will be designated HJA with the year of interview
23 Hardie D. "Exploring E.arly Jazz—the Origins and Evolution of the New Orleans Style"2002.

So, When Did Jazz First Appear?

It seems pretty clear that syncopated dance music began to appear in New Orleans around 1895. Some earlier dates have been suggested. Rose and Souchon[24] went as far as to state that Charles Galloway's band of 1889 might have been the first jazz band, though they were not prepared to support the suggestion, qualifying it by saying jazz developed over a period of thirty years. Marquis mentions Jack Laine claiming to have "ragged the tunes in 1885".[25] Manuel Perez said that popular demand for syncopated music around 1895 forced one popular dance band of the time to adopt the style, if rather reluctantly.[26] As we have seen, Charters suggested 1894/5 as the date when Bolden first played the blues at a dance at the Globe Hall.

Where was it Born?

Some early jazz writers spread the romantic notion that jazz was born in the bawdy houses of the Storyville red light district, but more recently it has become accepted that the dance bands did not perform in the bawdy houses where commonly the entertainment was provided by piano 'professors'. Small bands of musicians did operate in the cabarets that were dotted around in the district, but there was a ban on brass music being played there until around 1907.[27]

The transition from the conventional dance band to the Elemental Jazz orchestra occurred in the neighbourhood dances conducted in local halls built for dancing, meetings and other entertainments. Around 1834 Creole Friendly Societies began building these venues and the trend continued in the early years after the Civil War. By the 1880's similar buildings were being provided Uptown to cater for the large number of black (non-Creole) immigrants from the plantation belt. The early dance halls were too small to accommodate a sizeable brass band but the newer halls began to provide more adequate bandstands. This

---

24 Rose A. and Souchon E. "New Orleans Jazz—A Family Album" 1967 Louisiana State University Press, Baton Rouge p130
25 Marquis Op cit 1978/93 p 34 footnote 13.
26 Gushee L. "The Nineteenth Century Origins of Jazz" in Black Music Research Journal (BMRJ) Vol 14 No1 1994 pp1-24.
27 This ban is mentioned by Gushee in 'Pioneers of Jazz' p 28

permitted the employment of the mixed wind and string ensembles that were a feature of early jazz. Musicians employed at the time also mention neighbourhood dances being conducted on the lawn in vacant lots, in dairies and even ice cream parlours. The authorities also provided dance pavilions in some of the pleasure parks provided for use of the populace. It was in these dance music venues that Elemental Jazz prospered.

What's in a name?

If we had a birth certificate for the birth of jazz surely it would tell us its name. Genealogists would tell us that it not always easy to find the birth certificate even if we think we know the name of the child. If, for example, we searched the New Orleans registers of births deaths and marriages looking for Buddy Bolden we would not find him because he was christened as Charles Joseph Bolden. Similar difficulties were not uncommon there: Bunk Johnson was possibly born William Gary or Garie, and he himself referred to Peaco Forestier and Jimmy Scriggs—musicians better known as Alphonse Picou and James A. Palao. I suspect that he, and Jelly Roll Morton (aka Fernand Mouton or Ferdinand la Mothe) did not even know either their dates of birth or their exact parentage.[28]

So it was with jazz, which only acquired a name in 1917—about 20 years after its birth. Nevertheless, numerous musicians who played jazz after 1917 also performed before that. They often referred to the early music as 'syncopation' or 'swing', adding to the complication because one of its descendents was also popularly called Swing music in the 1930's.

Detractors called it 'ratty music'. They contrasted it with conventional popular song music, which in the early days they called 'classical music', further complicating our detective work.

When ragtime became popular around 1900 it rapidly became fashionable to call the syncopated music in New Orleans ragtime. (Thereafter almost every song published in the nation until about 1917 had rag or ragtime tagged on to it.) After 1917 everything was called jazz until around 1930 when it became Swing again.

---

[28] Interested readers will find much similar genealogical information on Mike Medding's website www.doctorjazz.co.uk

Because of these difficulties I have adopted the term suggested by Marquis—"Elemental Jazz"—to refer to the syncopated improvised music played during Bolden's musical career.[29]

---

[29] Some authorities call this music 'proto jazz' or refer to the history of the earliest jazz music as its 'prehistory'. I have rejected these usages as not reflecting accurately the state of development of the new music, which appears to have been well established by around 1900.

Chapter 2

The Social Dance Evening

Michié Préval li donnia gran bal. Li fait naig payé pou sauté in pé. Dansé Calinda, Boudoum Boudoum, Dansé Calinda, Boudoum Boudoum.[30]

Richard Collins searched the records of New Orleans black newspapers for information about the kind of music being played in New Orleans before the jazz revolution. Among other things he charted the development local social activities. He described the growth of a "social life centred on the dance or Balle"[31] that he felt was, in many ways, unique to New Orleans. This social life was facilitated by the construction of social halls, beginning around 1834. He indicated that, after the coming of the Americans in 1803, the Creole population banded together in friendly societies, like *Les Francs Amis*, that made their own recreational buildings, "partly as a response to repressive laws being enacted against Free Peoples of Colour"[32].

The Dance Halls

Before 1860 much of this activity was restricted to the Downtown sector, nominally occupied by the Creoles. However that changed after

---

[30] "Monsieur Preval, he gave a great Ball, He made the Negroes pay to get in to dance. Dance Calinda, Boudoum Boudoum etc."—La Calinda (traditional folk dance song)
[31] Collins R. "New Orleans Jazz—a Revised History" 1996 p14
[32] Collins op cit p66

the Civil War with the influx of free blacks to the Uptown suburbs formerly occupied by American and Immigrant groups.

Halls mentioned in the Creole period included those of *Les Jeunes Amis, Les Artisans* (later known as the *Artesian Hall,*) and *The Friends Of Hope Society* (*Hopes Hall*). He described the *Globe Hall* in St Peter St. as the best known Downtown dance hall for coloured people. He also listed non-Creole halls like the downtown headquarters of the Portuguese Lusitanos Society *(Lusitanian Hall)* functioning as early as 1859.

Other halls began to appear—*Werlein Hall*—*Economy Hall,* and with the end of slavery, buildings began to emerge Uptown to cater for the non-Creole blacks. In Bolden's time there were a considerable number of halls featuring neighbourhood or Friendly Society dances and Balls. Uptown there were the *Odd Fellows and Masonic Hall* on Perdido St. and the *Longshoreman's (or Jackson's) Hall* on Jackson Avenue; *Cottrell's Hall* on First St. *Providence Hall* was on South Liberty St. Others mentioned by Marquis include the *Electric Light Hall,* the *Love and Charity Hall, St. Elizabeth Hall* and the *Mississippi Valley Hall*. Downtown there were the *Perseverence Hall, Economy (or Cheapskate) Hall*[33] and of course, the *Globe Hall* mentioned by Sam Charters as the place where Bolden first played a blues for dancing.

Fig.3 Above: *Economy Hall* (aka *Cheapskate Hall*)

---

33 so called since "rich people didn't go there" see Marquis op cit p69

Collins stated that the older Downtown halls were small and had bandstands that were no more than balconies, or galleries, ten to fourteen feet high and some were unable to provide space for a large band. Those halls built at a later period had low bandstands 1 to 5 feet high, like modern bandstands.[34] He said that in the 1880's the *Werlein Hall* at the corner of Baronne and Perdido Streets could seat 1500.

Marquis established that Buddy Bolden's orchestra played all over the city including some of the rougher halls in the Downtown Section, though it did not play at better-class Creole Society halls like the *Franc Amis* or *Jeunes Amis*. It also played in halls across the river in Algiers. The band played regularly at the *Union Sons Relief Association Hall* at 1319 Perdido St—an old church that in Buddy's time, functioned as a Baptist church on Sundays and served as a dance hall on Saturday nights. It was known as the *Union Sons Hall* or, after the president of the Association, by the nickname *Kinney's Hall*. Later, because of its association with Bolden, it became known as the *Funky Butt Hall*.

Fig.4 Above: *Artisan (Artesian) Hall*—photo shows interior with small balcony bandstand.

---

34 Collins op cit p93

Dancin'

By the 1880's dancing was 'the most popular pastime in the Negro community.'[35] However, it was not like the wild performances of jigs, reels and jump ups common in the Negro juke[36] houses of the countryside. They were dancing Waltzes, Continentals, Prince Imperials, Mazurkas, Varieties, New Yorks, Lancers, Quadrilles, etc—all dances derived from the European tradition. This tradition lasted into the 1890's. As Collins put it:

> "... By 1890 when Bolden was still a boy and ragtime had not yet appeared on the scene New Orleans music for dancing, marching and all occasions resulted from a distinguished and lengthy experience."[37]

Our examination of music scores collected by the best-known conventional dance band of the late 1890's—John Robichaux's Orchestra, confirmed that this pattern continued in modified form into the 1900's. In particular, the appearance of the Two-step in the late 1880's required its addition to the repertoire.

Fig.5 above Artist's impression of conventional social dancing to fiddle and caller

---

35 Blassingame J.W. "Black New Orleans 1860-1880" pp145/6
36 sometimes spelled jook
37 Collins op cit p182

Robichaux played for the more conservative Creole dance audiences.[38] He usually tried to be up to date and acquired the following music published in 1896:

> 8 Marches
> 4 Quadrilles
> 3 Waltzes
> 2 Schottisches
> 2 Two-steps
> 2 Gavottes
> 2 Overtures
> 2 Lancers
> 1 One step
> 1 Song
> 1 "Characteristic piece'
> 3 others not classified

It should be noted that the Two-step was normally danced to march music.

Arrangements described as Cakewalks, Cakewalk Two-steps and Ragtime Two-steps began to appear among publications he acquired that were published in 1899, but there remained a significant number of Quadrilles, Waltzes, Polkas, Mazurkas, Schottisches and Two-steps among those from 1901 and later.

The arrival of the syncopating improvising bands of Bolden's time did not significantly change the structure of Creole dance evenings, and even in the Uptown district much of the old dancing was retained.

Cornet player Charlie Love[39] gave a graphic account of a typical Buddy Bolden social dance evening (25c at the door) that included the following dances:

> Waltz,
> Fast Two-step,
> Schottische
> Two-step polka
> Mazurka,

---

38 Analysis by Robyn Hardie 1997 based on previous survey conducted by Dr K. Koenig 1990
39 Recording 'The Music of New Orleans Vol IV' Folkways CD FA2464

> Quadrille introduction (8 bars—a hot piece)
> played for the dancers to get ready and line up
> for the Quadrille*
> Quadrille (5 figures)
>
> March, (played for the men to take their
> partners to the table for food.)^Ø
>
> Two-step polka,
> Slow drag,
> Polka-Mazurka
> Waltz,
> Two-step.
> Quadrille Intro (8 bars)
> Quadrille (5 figures)
>
> March (to table for food.)
> And so on until about 1am.

Love said that the band played this same type of repertoire at the *'Cooperatives Hall'* in Basin St and also at the *Globe Hall*, both Downtown venues.

He also mentioned the band playing a Ragtime Two-step, so at least one of the Two-step dances above could have been danced to a ragtime tune. Love said the band only played one or two rags an evening. There is no mention of a blues above, though the Slow drag could have been danced to a blues at the right tempo.

So they were still dancing the old dances with a few of the newer syncopated dances thrown in.

However the dance audience was not homogeneous. Marquis pointed out that Bolden adjusted his repertoire to suit the place and audience. He quoted a witness who was a member of the teenage girls

---

* Bunk Johnson said Bolden used what is now known as the first 8 bars of *Tiger Rag* to call the dancers for the Quadrille. June 12 1942 (Talking record Good Time Jazz LAG 545) In a recording made for the Library of Congress Jelly Roll Morton demonstrated the five figures of the same Quadrille as: Introduction, Waltz, Mazurka, Polka, and fast One-step. (Rounder CD1091)

Ø He said *Gettysburg March* was used but this was not published during Bolden's career. Later evidence has King Oliver's band as late as 1913 using a slow version of *High Society* for this purpose.

Blue Ribbon Social Club who said Bolden played for their Friday night dances around 1904.

> "The club paid five dollars for the hall and ten dollars for the band; ice cream and punch were served for refreshments. Bolden's musicians neither wore their hats on the bandstand nor did any drinking. They played Waltzes, Quadrilles, the Two-step and Slow drag—all dance music and no fast or jazzed up stuff—and no one sang lyrics as they might have at other dances. The kids liked Buddy and crowded around the bandstand; the band members in turn were polite, well-behaved and friendly."[40]

The refreshments appear to have been an important component of such dance evenings. Love said they had gumbo, roast, corn balls, ham sandwiches and then went for a drink ...

Fig.6 Above: *Union Son's Hall* or *Kinney's Hall* (aka *Funky Butt Hall*—famous as Buddy Bolden's regular hangout) as it may have appeared when it was the Greater St. Matthew's Baptist Church in the 1930's.

In contrast George Baquet who heard the band playing for a 15-cent dance at the *Oddfellow's Hall* said it was a very rough place where

---

40 Mrs Beatrice Alcorn in Marquis op cit p94

nobody took their hats off.[41] (It has been suggested that this was so they could get away quickly if trouble broke out.[42]) Apparently on such occasions they would sing crude words to tunes like *Funky Butt* and *Make Me a Pallet on the Floor*. Danny Barker said things got rough later in the evening after the more polite dances were finished and the sporting crowd began to arrive. For these rougher audiences the jump ups and low down blues were introduced into the repertoire.

There are some accounts of audience responses to these new Bolden innovations. Baquet described the reaction at the *Economy Hall* dance mentioned above:

> "Buddy held up his cornet, paused to be sure of his embouchure, then they played *Make Me a Pallet on the Floor*. Everybody got up quick, the whole place rose and yelled out, 'Oh, Mr Bolden, play it for us, Buddy, play it!'"[43]

Bill Matthews said that:

> "Everybody went crazy about Buddy Bolden when he'd blow a waltz, a schottische ... and them old low down blues."[44]

Trouble did break out at some of the rougher dances. Marquis identified a situation at the Union Sons Hall where two women were arrested for fighting (some believed they were fighting over Buddy), and Jelly Roll Morton claimed to have been present at a Bolden engagement where a murder occurred, probably at the *Economy Hall* in June 1902.[45]

In contrast, The Ladies of Providence and the Knights of Pleasure engaged "Prof. Bolden's Orchestra" for their Mardi Gras Ball at the *Providence Hall* on February 18 1903.[46]

It seems reasonable to conclude that while there was some variety among dance audiences around 1900 the dances performed were on the whole much the same as those performed earlier in the 1890's.

---

41 "Baquet on Bolden" Downbeat Vol VII March 1965 pp67/74
42 Mc Cusker J. on Bolden—DVD by Stefan Sargeant at www.stefansargeant.com
43 Shapiro and Hentoff "Hear Me Talkin' to Ya" 1955/66 p38
44 Interview at the Tulane Jazz Archive (HJA1959)
45 see Marquis op cit pp68 and 71
46 Marquis op cit p72

A number of witnesses mentioned the Quadrille as a feature of the dance evening. In fact, it was as we have seen, something of a high point of the entertainment irrespective of venue.

Early in its history New Orleans imported the Cotillion, a French variation of the Country Dance:

> The Cotillion was originally a dance of four couples, starting in square formation, who all danced simultaneously, sometimes as separate couples and sometimes together in chains, circles, or other patterns, resuming the square formation at the end of each sequence.[47]

By the 1870's its place had been taken by its descendant the Quadrille:

> The Quadrille, by contrast, had a very specific organization. Ideally, the classic Quadrille was distinguished from other square dances by having a particular series of five or six prescribed sequences, each different.[48]

However, over the years this prescribed form was diluted:

> "By the eighteen-fifties, Quadrilles commonly included round-dance episodes, generally a Polka or Galop, for eight or sixteen bars; even the Waltz was eventually included, although changing to 3/4 was often awkward."

By Bolden's time in New Orleans the Quadrille consisted of a series of dances played in turn—for example: Introduction, Waltz, Mazurka, Polka, Two-step, and popular tunes or operatic arias were often orchestrated to serve as Quadrille segments of various tempi.

Baby Dodds also described the introduction to the Quadrille:

> "In Quadrilles they have a little introduction that's two beats to the measure. It may be eight or twelve measures long and you stop. The introduction is for giving the dancers notice to get their partners. Then you've got another part you play, while they get lined up. And you play another part and they start dancing ... a Quadrille,

---

47 Hagert Thornton booklet accompanying CD 'Come and Trip It—Instrumental Dance music 1780-1920's' New Worlds records 80293-2 p7
48 Hagert op cit p7

which is a reel, they got about twelve parts to it. There is a Waltz and also a Mazooka."[49]

Jelly Roll Morton described it more colourfully:

> "Get your partners! Everybody get your partners! People would be rushing around the hall getting their partners. And maybe ... have maybe five minutes lapsed between that time. And of course they'd start it over again. And that was the first part."[50]

He then went on to demonstrate a Quadrille that included an introduction, waltz, mazurka, polka and what seems to be a fast jazz interpretation of the polka.

The style of dancing too seems to have varied with the audience. Thornton Haggert talking of the national scene described it thus:

> "... if in discussing all these matters of form I have given the impression that the old square dances were sedate and formal, please put it out of your mind. With the right performers, the Quadrille and the Cotillion were stomping, vigorous, rowdy, vulgar, abandoned, and exhilarating dances."[51]

So too with the musicians—it seems that the new improvising bands took musical liberties with dances like the Waltz, Mazurka and the Quadrille. One witness described a performance by an early band as follows:

> "He'd holler follow me and his bunch would rip into one of those old Quadrilles which induce so much lively jazz and he could play the *Anniversary Song** so the tears would run out of your eyes."[52]

Jelly Roll Morton who described the Uptown district in which Bolden lived as "kind of a loose section", described the above band as playing

---

49   Russel W. "New Orleans Style" 1994 p 24
50   Library of Congress recording 1648B
51   Hagert op cit p9
*   A Viennese Waltz
52   Louis Nelson Delille in Lomax "Mr Jelly Roll" 1952 p90 about Peyton's band—a Bolden predecessor.

a "low down" type of Quadrille for a "low down" audience. He also said that only the lower classes went to the dance halls.

The New Orleans piano player Armand Hug described the process:

> "The Quadrille was a proper dance, usually limited to a certain social strata, but the Uptown bands changed it to their own style. Jazz enabled the musician to let off steam. They played in the butler's pantry because they weren't allowed in the parlor. Some became brassy and egotistical as a compensation. They were impulsive, played blues and gutbucket. Depended on what people wanted to hear."[53]

This pattern does not appear to have changed much during the first ten years of jazz, and even later, the early dances were still being performed. Baby Dodds who was performing around 1910 wrote that on New Orleans dance dates they had to play Mazurkas, Quadrilles, Polkas and Schottisches:

> "There were certain dance halls in New Orleans where you had to play all those things. Some of the Creole people went only for that music. If you couldn't play them you didn't get the job."[54]

Strangely, there is not much information about the type of dancing performed to the newer syncopated music and blues though Baby Dodds did comment on the latter:

> "In New Orleans we used to play the blues and the lowest type of dancers used to love such things. They were played very slow, and fellows and their girl friends would stand almost still and just make movements ... Those are really sporting numbers, which were played in the sporting houses or when sporting people would get together."[55]

It is unfortunate that our conception of jazz music for dancing was formed from recordings made after 1917, when the more traditional dances had disappeared from the national dance scene. The jazz music

---

53 Marquis op cit p101
54 Dodds and Gara "The Baby Dodds Story" 1959/1992p10
55 Dodds and Gara op cit p29

of the 1920's and later became limited to fast and slow performances in common time for dances like the One-step, Charleston and Foxtrot, formulae unknown in the days of Elemental Jazz. Recordings made at that time give the impression that blues and stomps were the foundation of jazz dancing. This was far from the truth. If you had happened to enter the *Funky Butt Hall* on a Saturday evening in 1900 you might have heard a blues, but just as likely they would have been dancing an exuberant Waltz or jazzed up Quadrille.

'Low class' dancing

Outside the dance halls music was provided in beer halls and cabarets located both in the red light district and neighbourhoods uptown.

Asbury recorded the emergence of barrelhouses, concert-saloons and dance halls in the 1860's. He stated that the barrelhouses and concert-saloons were introduced by: "Northern riff raff, which flocked to the city in the wake of Farragut's victorious fleet."

The barrelhouses were drinking places, (he called them "guzzle shops",) which occupied a long narrow room with a row of barrels on one side where customers could fill a mug with beer from the spigots of the barrels.

The concert-saloon or dance hall, the forerunner of the modern nightclub, provided a dance-floor upon which "the pleasure seekers might kick up their heels to the music of a tinny piano or squeaky fiddle." Shows, often including posing models, or dances like 'Can can' and 'Clodoche' were sometimes provided. He listed many such places including the St Nicholas, The Gem, the New El Dorado, and the Amsterdam Dance House and quoted numerous incidents that defined them as bawdy, ruffianly, violent and venal.[56] This trend continued. Donald Marquis was able to list a score of their descendants, beer halls and saloons of various types, operating around Rampart St. and Perdido St between 1895 and 1910.[57][58]

Numerous cabarets and beer halls operated in the red light district in Bolden's time and gradually music was provided by string bands and other small combinations including wind instruments. Dances in these

---

56 Asbury H. "The French Quarter" 1936/1981 p244 ff
57 Marquis op cit p53
58 extract from Hardie D. "The Ancestry of Jazz—a Musical Family History".

smaller establishments were apparently quite different from those of the dance halls. Gushee provided evidence that couple dances like the Turkey Trot, Grizzly Bear, Todelo and Texas Tommy probably derived from earlier Afro American vernacular dances like the jig and Juba were popular in the tenderloin as early as 1890.[59]

> "In the Grizzly Bear, the couple, leaning heavily on each other and locked in a bear hug, lumbered in a slight crouch from foot to foot, two-steps to the bar. My guess is that it was originally a simple, slow, and sexual dance (the kind you do up against a wall)[60]

The Turkey Trot was a faster dance probably also derived from earlier traditional jigs and breakdown dances.

The Bands

Early accounts of dances in the Creole dance halls refer to the musicians as 'bands of music' and it is generally assumed these were small string bands. Collins concluded that until the mid 19th Century, dance music in New Orleans, as elsewhere was provided by string bands comprised of violins, violas, mandolins and guitars. He suggested that larger stringed instruments—cellos, bass violins and pianos were only used on jobs where there was a large enough bandstand.[61]

After the Civil War there was a flourishing brass band movement in the city (and elsewhere in the country.)[62] However the brass bands that generally comprised 12 or more players could not be employed in the smaller dance halls.

Collins detected a change in 1881 when he found a newspaper reference to a band called the Midnight Revellers organising themselves into a "tin band". He described the tin band as a hybrid band of brass woodwind and strings that he believed became possible because the introduction of "the Albert System 13 keyed clarinet":

> "The people of New Orleans were accustomed to hearing the soft music of string bands or the more sonorous

---

59 Gushee BMRJ 1994 Vol 14 No1 pp20/21
60 Hagert op cit p22
61 Collins op cit p93
62 see Hardie D. "The Ancestry of Jazz: A Musical Family History" Chapter 7

> sound of the brass bands. To their ears this hybrid band had a tinny sound.... As late as the 1950's some older New Orleans brass band musicians still referred to this type of band as a tin band."[63]

Collins believed this was a New Orleans innovation but, as I have pointed out in an earlier work, this transition also occurred elsewhere.[64] Collins gave as an example the well known Silver Leaf Band that began adding brass instruments before 1890, though he points out that in the 1880's string bands and brass bands were still the most widely accepted. In the five years leading up to the birth of jazz, dance music was increasingly provided by the so-called 'tin bands' though string bands maintained a strong position in the market.[65] However by around 1895 mixed bands like the John Robichaux' Orchestra were gaining a foothold. The composition of the groups varied. In 1896 Robichaux had two violins, two cornets, clarinet, slide trombone, bass violin and trap drums, and many of the popular publisher's stock arrangements of dance tunes provided parts for this type of group. This group must have been too large for many dance engagements and in the 1900's he pruned it down.

Buddy Bolden began playing cornet with a string band around 1895 and, over time, added trombone, clarinet and trap drums. Soon the Elemental Jazz orchestra settled into a regular seven piece format that can be seen in photographs taken during the first twenty years of jazz: violin, cornet, clarinet, valve trombone, Spanish guitar, bass violin and trap drums.

If you had gone to the *Union Son's Hall* for a Saturday night dance in 1900 the chances are that this type of 'Tin Band' is what you would have danced to, but it was no longer tinny, but loud and brassy.

---

63 Collins op cit pp 170/171
64 Hardie D, "Exploring Early Jazz; the Origin and Evolution of the New Orleans Style". P20
65 see Hardie D, "Exploring Early Jazz; the Origin and Evolution of the New Orleans Style". Chapter 2

Chapter 3

The Creators of Jazz

"He teaches himself his own way about it, picking up sounds native to his neighbourhood and class; the street songs, the soul steeped hymns of the Baptist Church, the blues from corner guitar pickers."[66]

—Frederick Turner

Around 1890 a sea change began in New Orleans dance music. Perhaps it had begun a little earlier than that, and it swelled until the jazz revolution was well established towards the end of the decade.

Buddy Bolden was 13 in 1890. Charlie "Sweet Lovin'" Galloway was 21, and he had a dance band. Galloway had suffered from polio and had to use crutches. Reports indicate that when he was about 16, in 1885, he was a street musician playing his guitar for tips. His partner in this endeavour was Jefferson 'Brock" Mumford another crippled guitar player, then only 12 years old.

This street music theme occurs again and again in the early history of jazz. It appears that street music provided an opportunity for the vernacular music played in the streets and juke houses of the countryside to influence music in the city. In his autobiography, Pops Foster described the street bands that played for coins in the street. He said most of the players came 'out of the woods' or from some little town'.[67]

---

[66] Turner F. "Remembering Song: Encounters with the New Orleans Jazz Tradition" 1994 p26
[67] Foster P. "Pops Foster" 1971 p61

Galloway soon had a string band that played for dances and parties and by 1895 he ran a barber shop on South Rampart St.[68] Galloway's barbershop served as a hangout for musicians and apparently also as an informal booking agency. This was a musical tradition that may have had roots in Shakespeare's England but in the South, where Jim Crow segregationist laws denied blacks access to many social facilities, the local barbershop was 'an accessible and welcoming hang out'.[69]

> "Black neighbourhood barbershops came to serve as social halls, conservatories and rehearsal studios for local singers and musicians of every description."[70]

Rose and Souchon suggested that Galloway's band of 1889 was the first they heard of that was referred to as a jazz band.[71] An even earlier date was suggested by a witness who said that:

> "...around 1885 Negroes formed combos of clarinet cornet trombone and bull fiddle, which "jazzed up" the popular tunes of the day"[72]

Another early bandleader Louis Ned, born 1858, was said to have played 'skiffle music' in the streets very early.

---

68 Marquis D. op ct p40
69 see more extensive account of barbershops in the South in Abbott and Seroff "Out of Sight: the Rise of African American Popular Music"
70 Abbott L. and Seroff D. "Out of Sight—The Rise of African American Popular Music"
71 Rose and Souchon "New Orleans Jazz—A Family Album" p130
72 Gushee L. "Pioneers of Jazz" p321

Fig.7 Above: New Orleans street band before 1900, mandolin, guitar and string bass. The bass violin player is Albert Glenny who later played with Galloway and Buddy Bolden.

Syncopation

During the first five years of the decade syncopated dance music began to appear. Manuel Perez saw it beginning around 1893 as a: 'syncopated evolution' beginning in "vocal groups of young Creoles, such as those of the spasm band that retained the rhythmic aspect of all badly digested music".[73]

This is an interesting observation. The Spasm Band members are usually considered white, not Creole, but Jelly Roll Morton used the term more broadly:

---

[73] Gushee L. "The Nineteenth Century Origins of Jazz" 1994 Black Music Research Journal 9 Vol 14 No1 (BMRJ) p17

> "... a lot of bad bands we called spasm bands, played any jobs they could get in the streets. They did a lot of ad-libbing in ragtime style with different solos in succession, not in a regular routine but just as one guy would get tired and let another musician have the lead."[74]

Morton also described small groups of serenading street singers. Another source said that:

> "(Bunk Johnson) used to buy Jack Johnson—a cheap New Orleans wine—for the little boys in the sidewalk string bands"[75]

So it appears this street string band tradition continued to thrive throughout the period during which Elemental Jazz was evolving. They were three, four or five piece bands using violin or mandolin, guitar, string bass and sometimes a wind instrument and many musicians first played in such a group.[76]

George Filhé who played trombone with John Robichaux before 1900 and later with Perez' Imperial Orchestra stated that around 1892 the younger musicians began to 'swing' while the older musicians used 'lots of Mexican music'. He said that at that time:

> "The Cousto-Desdunes Orchestra played jazz, would always swing the music, that was their novelty. Played Quadrilles and schottisches straight."[77]

This appears to indicate that dances like the emerging Two-step would have been played in a syncopated fashion.

Manuel Perez who clearly did not approve said that after 1895 another well known Creole Orchestra—the Tio–Doublet Orchestra reluctantly:

> "Let themselves be tempted by the infatuation of the audiences and went along with the new music."[78]

---

74 Lomax A. op cit p61
75 Charters op cit p34
76 Gushee BMRJ article above p 15
77 Gushee BMRJ p16
78 Gushee BMRJ p17

Uptown

By 1894 Charlie Galloway had formed his band into a 'tin band' reinforcing the earlier string band with valve trombone, cornet and clarinet, and they were playing for dancing at the Masonic Hall, on Rampart at Perdido.

In 1894 Buddy Bolden (then 17) started learning cornet and 'the rudiments of music' from Manuel Hall, who was a friend of his mother.[79][80] It has been suggested he may also have had accordion lessons from Algiers musician Felix Palao.[81] He apparently made rapid progress and began playing part-time dates as a professional musician, notably with Galloway's band and that of accordion player Charles Peyton—a group noted for hot performance of the Quadrille.

Fig.8 Above Left: Buddy Bolden (cornet) and Jefferson (Brock) Mumford (guitar) ca 1905 Right: Manuel Perez (cornet) and Jimmy Brown (bass) of the Imperial Orchestra ca 1908

---

79 Marquis D. op cit p 38
80 Buddy Bolden's grand parents were slaves owned by a William Walker, who sold his plantation to one of his neighbours and went to New Orleans (about 1865). There he bought a carrying business, which he ran from 354 Calliope Street near the Railroad Depot. Gustavus Bolden,
Frances Bolden and their three children went to New Orleans with William Walker and lived in a small house behind the Walker residence at 354 Calliope Street. They 'made the transition from trusted slaves to trusted employees' and continued to live at the Walker property. Buddy's father Westmore Bolden also worked for Walker as a drayman.
81 Gushee L. "Pioneers of Jazz" *p29*

As he progressed Bolden began using musicians from Galloway's band, including Galloway himself on guitar, to accept bookings in his own name.[82] He probably took over leadership of Galloway's band in 1895 or 1896. Marquis stated that by 1897 the style and organization of Bolden's band was taking shape.[83] This seems a reasonable suggestion.

Sam Charters said that the former street musician Charlie Galloway, introduced some of the popular street songs to the dance orchestras:

> "Galloway and Bolden seem to have been the first men to use musical material from their racial background for orchestral playing. Galloway lived on St. Mary Street, Bolden on 1st Street, not too far away. To play any of the songs of the uptown neighborhoods an instrumental group would have to restate the melody in terms of some instrument, and find harmonic patterns to fit the melody. It is possible that the two of them—Bolden, a cornet player, and Galloway, a guitar player established these patterns for a few simple tunes playing together in the early 1890's."[84]

While there is no evidence of Bolden himself having been a street player it was widely accepted by contemporaries that he was the first to play the blues for dancing. As we have seen, Charters said it was at the Globe Hall in 1894 or 1895, but this dating cannot be confirmed. Nevertheless this innovation proved popular with at least part of the dance audience.

By 1897 Bolden appears to have melded the syncopated performance style developed in the early 1890's with elements from street music sources and the blues into the performances of his orchestra, but there was another new element. Bolden's family belonged to the Baptist church and there is strong evidence that Bolden drew on the rich tradition of holy roller hymns, spirituals, and shouts in establishing the new style. By 1900 the charismatic Bolden was feted as the man who invented the 'Hot Blues' and he became known as King Bolden.[85]

---

82 Marquis D. op cit p 42
83 Marquis D. op cit p 43.
84 Charters S. op cit p13
85 Richard Collins expressed an alternative view: "Alphonse Picou, the famous New Orleans clarinettist, was of the opinion that he was the first musician to introduce the blues into New Orleans Music as a sort of novelty" Collins op cit p6

While it is easy to see how Bolden was influenced by church music it is not clear where he came into contact with the blues. Jelly Roll Morton said that the blues was being played in the New Orleans tenderloin in the 1880's, before he was born.

Possibly Bolden at 17 had heard the blues in the red-light district and decided to include it in his dance repertoire. More likely, some of the tunes adapted from the street performers were blues. Contemporaries also said that he stole tunes from the junk man, who played haunting blues on a children's tin horn, and adapted them for his band.

Bolden's role appears to have been to gather the various elements, syncopation, ad-lib performance, street songs, spirituals and the blues to establish a way of playing that was recognized by audiences and other musicians as something different. A consistent style emerged and other bands rapidly adopted it. By 1900 there were nine or ten bands playing the new music.

Fig.9 Above Left: Joe Petit founder of the Olympia Orchestra (ca 1903) with his valve trombone. Right: Jimmy Johnson who played bass violin with the Bolden Orchestra

From the above summary it appears that jazz had a gestation period during the first five years of the 1890's and that a number of different performers contributed to its genesis.

Bands like the Cousto (Coustaut)-Desdunes Orchestra[86] and the Tio-Doublet Orchestra derived from the conventional Creole orchestral tra-

---

86 Led by cornetists Manuel and Sylvester Coustaut and Violinist Dan Desdunes

dition and it is unusual to hear of them performing in a proto-jazz style. George Filhé played trombone with the Cousto–Desdunes Orchestra around 1892[87] so he should have known how they played, though 1892 appears very early to be playing jazz as a feature. The Tio-Doublet (Dublais) Orchestra began life as a small String Orchestra before 1889. A.L. Tio and Anthony Doublet (Dublais) played violins, Prof W.J. Nickerson viola, and Paul Dominguez Sr. bass violin. These were well-trained, distinguished musicians of the old school, so their reluctance to swing the music is understandable. (The dance orchestra apparently included Anthony Page on valve trombone and Dee Dee Chandler drums.) Brian Wood[88] says they played regularly at the *Francs Amis Hall* around 1889.[89]

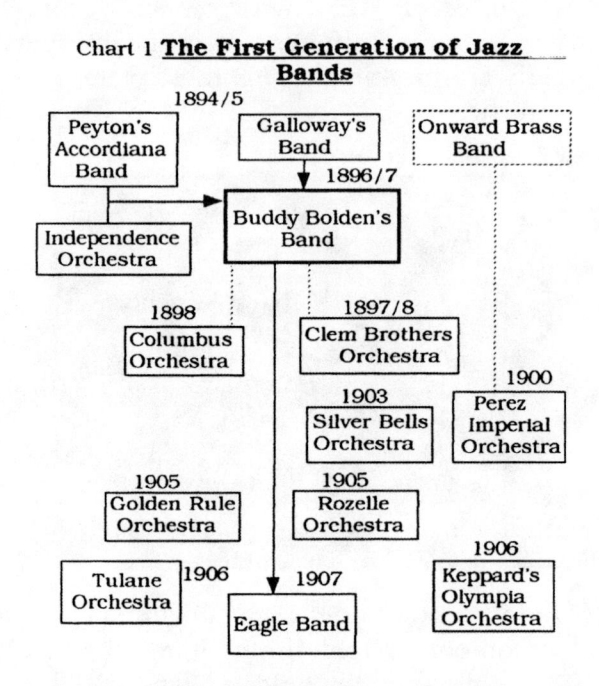

Chart 1 The First Generation of Jazz Bands

```
1894/5
Peyton's          Galloway's        Onward Brass
Accordiana        Band              Band
Band                    │
   │               1896/7
   └──────────→  Buddy Bolden's
Independence     Band
Orchestra
                        │
   1898           1897/8
Columbus         Clem Brothers
Orchestra        Orchestra
                                    1900
                  1903              Perez
                  Silver Bells      Imperial
                  Orchestra         Orchestra

   1905           1905
Golden Rule      Rozelle
Orchestra        Orchestra
                                    1906
   Tulane  1906   1907              Keppard's
Orchestra        Eagle Band         Olympia
                                    Orchestra
```

Chart 1 Above: showing the best known bands of the first jazz generation[90]

---

87 Charters op cit p 29
88 Wood B. "The Song For Me" 2003 Under alphabetical bio entry
89 Note the trap drum set was not invented in 1889 but introduced by Chandler in 1896. If he played with the Tio-Doublet orchestra before that, he either played only snare drum or employed a double-drumming technique.
90 Originally published in "Exploring Early Jazz—the Origins and and Evolution of the New Orleans Style."

Galloway's Orchestra derived from a different tradition. Musicians like bass players Bob Lyons, Albert Glenny and bass horn player Wallace Collins who played with him also had street music experience.

The dates given above, relying as they do on early memories may give a false appearance of certainty, though they are to some extent consistent. It appears that the syncopated street music style of the early 1890's began to percolate into the dance halls before 1895 and that by 1897 Bolden's band was performing in a style that added improvisation and the blues to the performance of a repertoire of conventional dances that still included the older square dances, Waltzes, Polkas and Mazurkas.

The First Elemental Jazz Bands

During the decade 1897/1907 a number of bands were formed that took up the new style and developed it. Some of them, like Alphonse Picou's Independence orchestra, that had similar personnel to Peyton's Orchestra, had roots in earlier combinations. Valve trombonist Joe Petit, founder of the Olympia Orchestra, was particularly active in forming bands, and the Frank Brothers Alcide and Bab Frank contributed to a number of groups.

Some more conventional groups, among them the Imperial Orchestra associated with Manuel Perez and violinist James A. Palao, retained something of the old style. Established musical families like the Piron family, the Bocage family and the Manetta family began to associate themselves tentatively with the new music.

Ragtime Appears

Gushee has suggested that the impetus for the change to syncopated two-beat music was the introduction of the Two-step around 1890. He pointed out that the dance—originally performed to marches like Sousa's *Washington Post March* and danced in 6/8 time had, by the end of the decade, become the dance to which ragtime[91] was played.[92]

---

91 Ragtime music is usually composed in duple time—commonly 2/4 or in cut common time.
92 Gushee BMRJ p19

It is important to note that the first ragtime compositions, so named, were not published until 1896. As indicated in the previous chapter, ragtime compositions did not appear in the Robichaux collection before 1897 when an arrangement of *Mississippi Rag—Two-step* (significantly in 2/4 time) appeared. It cannot therefore be argued that ragtime, as we know it from the music of Scott Joplin and others of the classical school, played any part in the formulation of the Elemental Jazz style.

How then do we explain the apparently pejorative comments by Jelly Roll Morton when he said that the street bands were playing 'in ragtime style'? As is often the case we cannot be sure of the precise dating of the music to which he referred, though he appears to have been talking about early teenage experiences.[93] Unfortunately clouds of controversy obscure his birth date. If, as most commonly believed, he were born in 1890 he would have been seven years old in 1897 and 12 in 1902[94]. If he were born in 1885, as sometimes suggested, he would have been 8 in 1892 and 12 in 1897 old enough to participate in street music and 17 when he claimed he himself invented jazz in 1902.[95]

In any case, he could not have had a deep knowledge of Classical Rags in 1897,[96] so he must have been talking about something else, a style of playing that to him meant ragtime.

This can only make any sense if we accept the view that there was a stream of ragtime like music that predated the first Classic ragtime publications—the so-called 'folk ragtime', and that the street musicians of New Orleans were performing in folk ragtime style.

The best evidence suggests that before the first published rags appeared there were numerous performers playing folk piano ragtime called jig piano in jook houses and beer halls throughout the country, and in New Orleans, in the bordellos.

> "The extraordinary ragtime at Nashville Tennessee, for instance, could well be called a school of Folk Rag composition. There is a consistent style here and an ebullient

---

[93] We will strike this problem again in relation to his descriptions of the Bolden style.

[94] See "Jelly Roll Morton An Essay in Genealogy" by Peter Hanley at http://www.doctorjazz.co.uk/genealogy.html#genjelly

[95] Morton claimed he was playing in string bands at the age of seven (Lomax op cit p6)

[96] Joplin's first rag was published in 1899.

mix of both black folk sources and white Tennessee hill music, a distinctly Southern fried concoction."[97]

At the same time, individual street musicians and string bands were performing jigs, jump-ups and elemental blues music.

While both early jazz and written ragtime appeared at the same time at appears both ultimately derived from the same stream of vernacular music. Ragtime of the Joplin school sought to apply the rules of conventional composition to the piano jigs of the 1890's. At the same time, in contrast, the improvising musicians of New Orleans were applying earlier informal syncopated performance practices and repertoire to conventional dance music.

---

[97] Jasen and Tichenor "Rags and Ragtime: a Musical History" 1978 p22

Chapter 4

The Repertoire Part 1
Popular Songs and Rags

"Their tunes came from a million sources. Many of them were stolen from old marches (*High Society* for instance) and were the leader's interpretation of the old marches. Because he couldn't read, the band played it different from the original."

—Jack Weber[98]

In late 2004 I convened a repertory orchestra to explore the repertoire of Elemental Jazz, and present concert performances with original instrumentation, in a style that, as far as possible, recreates the sounds of Elemental Jazz. I was fortunate in being able to obtain the assistance of some of Australia's foremost performers in the New Orleans Style. The group was rather optimistically named The Buddy Bolden Revival Orchestra.

In order to obtain authentic repertoire it was necessary to research the music of the period. It was decided that the best approach was to take as a starting point what was known about the actual repertoire of the Buddy Bolden Orchestra. We were greatly assisted in this by work done by New Orleans writer Carlos 'Froggy' May and published on his website[99], and by an extended list published on the Internet by

---

98 Shapiro and Hentoff op cit p59
99 www.angelfire.com/la/carlosmay—this website does not now appear to be functioning.

Ingemar Wågerman of the Gota River Jazzmen[100] in preparation for a CD entitled '... thought I Heard Buddy Bolden Play'. These provided a beginning.

A number of items that proved to have been published after 1907, or were otherwise of uncertain validity were eliminated from our final list. One or two additional items published during Bolden's career, known to have been widely performed at the time, were added to the final repertoire.

Table 1. Buddy Bolden's Repertoire (Revised)

Popular Songs
Any Rags
Don't Go Way Nobody
Emancipation Day
Home Sweet Home
Ida
Idaho
If the Man in the Moon Were a Coon
Lazy Moon
Mr Johnson Turn Me Loose
Shoo Skeeter Shoo
Under the Bamboo Tree*
Wait til the Sun Shines Nellie

Traditional Dance Tunes
La Praline (Quadrille)
Moonwinks (Mazurka
Over the Waves – Waltz*
Sweet Adeline – Schottische*
In High Society – Slow March to the supper table*

Piano Ragtime
Bowery Buck (Turpin)
Frog Legs Rag (Scott)
Maple Leaf Rag (Joplin)
Palm Leaf Rag (Joplin)
Panama Rag (Seymour)

Dance Songs/Jump Ups
All the Whores Like the Way I Ride
Funky Butt
Get Out of Here
If You Don't Shake
Makin Runs
My Bucket's Got a Hole In it
The Old Cow Died (And Old Brock Cried)

Blues
Careless Blues
Get Your Big Fat Leg Off Me
If You Don't Like My Potatoes Why Do You Dig so Deep?
Make Me a Pallet on the Floor
Salty Dog
2/19 Blues

Spirituals
Go Down Moses
Ride On King Jesus
Run Nigger (Strumpet) Run (From Spiritual Run Mary Run)

*Not in original list- added by author to improve representativeness of dance types

Table 1 Above: Revised Bolden Repertoire 1897/1907

---

100 www.geocities.com/BourbonStreet/Canal/2032/gotariver.english.html

There were some Classical Ragtime compositions on the list that some authorities contended could not have been played by Bolden, but I decided to include them to test the contention and to adequately represent the range of tunes played by bands of the time.

I was able to obtain original published scores, later transcriptions, or recorded performances of the majority of the compositions listed. Original scores were obtained from Internet sources and from a number of correspondents, including the Tulane University Jazz Archive. My colleagues provided valuable assistance in interpreting, transcribing and/or arranging original material, some of which was recovered in very sketchy form. A few items have proved impossible to track down, though efforts continue.

Much of this repertoire was played through in rehearsal and a considerable number of compositions performed in concert. However, in the process of accumulating the musical material and preparing it for performance, numerous questions about the music of the Elemental Jazz period were raised.

Analysing The Repertoire

It quickly became obvious that there was a lack of correspondence between the tune list and the list of dance types regularly performed by the Uptown bands and listed in Chapter 2. Out of 40 odd compositions only 2 (*Moonwinks Mazurka* and *La Praline Quadrille*) were composed to suit the conventional dances that predominated at the time. Some of the other tunes could perhaps have been adapted. *Lazy Moon*, for example, could perhaps have been played as a Schottische. There were no Polkas or Waltzes in the original list.[101]

Quite a number of the so called popular songs listed may have been suited to the performance of the Ragtime Two-step and probably some of the faster vernacular dance songs (jump ups) could have been employed for that purpose. When combined with the vernacular blues this latter group of vulgar dance songs made up the largest segment of the repertoire, and this is clearly the grouping of tunes that includes the street songs adapted by Galloway and Bolden for dance performance.

---

101 Two further tunes, *Over the Waves* and *Sweet Adeline*, which were known to have been played by early bands, were added as typical of waltz and schottische and *High Society* was included as the march to the supper table.

The Popular Songs

In Bolden's time the musicians would have called the 12 popular songs included in the repertoire 'classical numbers'. Significantly, six of them were Coon Songs, and five sentimental songs. One was a March, and one of the Coon Songs (*Shoo Skeeter Shoo*) an advertising ditty. In this respect the balance of compositions appears to accurately reflect the prevailing public tastes.

Since the 1820's, so called Parody Songs, that mimicked and lampooned the behaviour and language of slaves and free blacks had been popular especially on the Minstrel and vaudeville stages. With the development of the music publishing industry in the 1880's piano scores of this type of material began to be published and around 1890 a new era of popularity began for what began to be known as the Coon Song.[102] After 1896 they would have been called ragtime songs.

Coon Songs

Typically the verse of a Coon Song would be written in parody dialect. This excerpt from the first verse of *Mr Johnson Turn Me Loose (1896)* is a good example:

"T'other eb-'ning eb-'ry-ting was still, Oh! babe....
De moon was climb-in down be-hind de hill, Oh! babe ...
T'ough eb-'ry bo-dy was a sound a-sleep,
But a old man Johnson was a on His Beat, Oh! babe ...
I went down in-to a nig-ger crap game,
Where de coons were a gambling wid a might and main
T'ought I'd a be a sport and be dead game,
I gambled my mon-ey and I wasn't to blame ..."

This song was composed by stage performer Ben Harney who claimed to be the inventor of the Ragtime Song, which he introduced to the New York stage in the 1890's. It is believed to be one of the first written compositions to combine elements of blues and ragtime. Harney called it a Coon Novelty

It tells of a hapless 'coon' caught loitering in someone's chicken yard. He begs his captor to set him free; not put him in the calaboose.

---

102 See Hardie D. "The Ancestry of Jazz—a Musical Family History" Chapter 9

Musicologist Peter Van Der Merwe argued that Mister Johnson is a member of the same tune family as the traditional folk song *Pretty Polly* and "also very like the bluesy spiritual *Motherless Children.*"[103]

Some of the other items in the Coon Song list have special significance:

1. <u>Don't Go Way Nobody</u> is remembered as the tune Buddy Bolden played to start his evening dances. It is still played by New Orleans bands. Now they usually play only the chorus, which appears to have lost its original meaning. Furthermore, inspection of the original melody showed that the chorus is now played somewhat differently from the original. Also the words revealed its origins:

   "I've worked out on the le-vee front, right in the broiling sun.
   I've worked on eve-'ry steamboat, too, that ever dare to run.
   Worked at the docks from morn 'til night and burnt out lots of men. When the whistle blew to knock off, the boss would yell out then: 'Don't go way no-body! Don't nobody leave!
   'cause I need somebody to help me I believe
   Stay right here and be nice.
   I don't want to tell you twice.
   Don't go w ay e, no-body!
   Don't nobody leave!

   This is certainly based on a Coonjine Song[104]—the type of song sung by the roustabouts who loaded the paddle steamers that plied the Mississippi.[105] Typically they were complaints about a nigger-driving boss, usually referred to as Mr Charlie, who overworked or cheated the roustabouts.[106]

   It is perhaps not a typical Coon Song. It seems Bolden adapted it, possibly from an original score. Charlie Love said that in Bolden's time it was called *"Don't Go Way Nobody—Stay and Have a Good Time"*.

---

103 Van der Merwe P. "The Origins of the Popular Style" Clarendon Press 1989/1992 p280/1
104 "...'coonjine' is used on the Mississippi River for a peculiar motion used apparently to lighten or hasten the labor of loading and unloading (cargo)"—Abbott and Seroff op cit p309
105 see Hardie D. "The Ancestry of Jazz" pp 115/6
106 see Hardie D "The Ancestry of Jazz' p113

2. <u>*Any Rags*</u> was published by Thomas Allen in 1902. It appears that, like *Don't Go Way Nobody, Any Rags* may have been derived from an earlier folk music source.

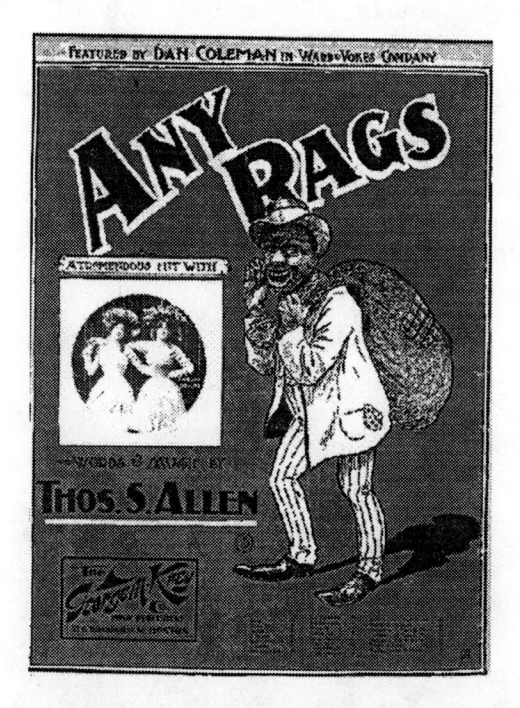

Fig.10 Above: Cover illustration from the piano score of *Any Rags*.

It has the usual banal dialect Coon Song verse but the chorus has words that have strong similarities to a Junk man's call recorded by folk music collector John Work:

> *"Rag man, bone man, comes your way,*
> *Rag man, bone man, bottles today,*
> *Well a big fat rag picker standing out here,*
> *Crying; rags and bones and bottles today."*[107]

The chorus of *Any Rags* reads:

> *"Any rags?—Rags?*
> *Any rags, any bones, any bottles today,*

---

107 Work J. "American Negro Folk Songs"

There's a big black rag picker coming this way
Any rags?—Rags?
Any rags, any bones, any bottles today,
It's the same old story in the same old way."

Witnesses said that Bolden stole the music of the Junk man to make tunes for his band. Others said he played *Any Rags*
The other Coon Songs in the repertoire were:

If the Man in the Moon were a Coon (1905)
Shoo Skeeter Shoo (1905)
Under the Bamboo Tree (1902)
Emancipation Day (?)

These are typical Ragtime Songs of the turn of the early 1900's.

If the Man in the Moon Were a Coon, published in 1903, has words people would now find objectionable but this sort of thing seems to have been acceptable in Bolden's time.

Fig.11 Above: Cover illustration from the piano score of *Shoo Skeeter Shoo* shows parodic style typical of Coon Song publications.

Shoo Skeeter Shoo is believed to have been composed as a reaction to a mosquito plague in New Orleans and, some believe Bolden played it to warn citizens of the danger of fever from mosquito bites.

The tune of *Under the Bamboo Tree* by Bob Cole and J. Rosamond Johnson was apparently adapted from the melody of the spiritual *Nobody Knows the Trouble I Have Seen*. It sold 400,000 copies.[108]

I had some difficulty with the song listed as *Emancipation Day*. This is often assumed to be the exuberant song (march) *On Emancipation Day* published by Wil. Marion Cook in 1902. However I found scores of two previous compositions entitled *Emancipation Day*; one by C. St. John in 1879, and a still earlier one by C.L.Stout and D. Braham in 1876.[109] They are celebrations of the Emancipation of the slaves in 1864 at the end of the Civil War. All retain Coon Song elements. I concluded that Bolden would be most likely to have heard the 1902 publication.

Sentimental Songs

Sentimental ballads dominated early popular music publications from before the time of Stephen Foster (in the 1840s and 50's). They continued to form a significant proportion of popular publications right up to Bolden's time, and this is reflected in the repertoire.

---

108 Morgan L. and Barlow W."From Cakewalks to Concert Halls" 1992 p 60
109 Apparently there was another by minstrel performer Sam Lucas.

Fig.12 Above sheet music cover *Wait 'till the Sun Shines Nellie*

These songs along with the Coon Songs were often introduced via stage shows and later they were sold as piano sheet music and or orchestral arrangements.

The oldest published song played by Bolden is undoubtedly *Home Sweet Home* the tune of which was composed by Englishman Sir Henry Bishop in 1821 for his opera *Clari, the Maid of Milan*. In 1823 it was given the present words by American poet John Howard Payne, and became one of the most popular parlour songs of the late 19th Century. At the better class venues in which he performed Bolden apparently would close the evening's performance with *Home Sweet Home*.

The inclusion of sentimental tunes like *Ida Sweet as Apple Cider* (1903), *Idaho* (1906), *Lazy Moon* (1903) and *Wait till the Sun Shines Nellie* (1905) indicate that although Bolden's audiences were apparently enthusiastic about the rough syncopated 'jump ups' and blues the band had introduced they also wanted to hear popular hit tunes of the day.

Like the Coon Songs, they often have banal and musically unmemorable verses, and it seems likely Bolden's audiences would have been satisfied with instrumental adaptations of the chorus. Who now remembers the verse of *Ida* or that of *Wait till the Sun Shines Nellie?*

Charlie Love remembered that sometimes the Bolden band would sit on the steps outside of the hall where Robichaux was playing in order to hear some of the newest tunes.[110]

Conventional Dance Tunes

Fortunately two conventional dance compositions were mentioned by witnesses as having been played by the Bolden band, though from the composition of the typical dance programmes outlined in a previous chapter there should have been many more. Presumably witnesses who were interviewed in the 1940's or later recalled only those numbers played in duple time, as tunes of that type then comprised the whole of the recorded jazz repertoire. Other sources suggest that at least until 1912 there must have been a significant demand for dances in three four or six eight time.

Around 1900, dancing the **Quadrille** was the highlight of the New Orleans dance evening. Only one Quadrille appears in the Bolden repertoire though Bunk Johnson only mentions the Introduction to the Quadrille as having been played by Bolden. This was the Quadrille known variously as *La Praline* or *La Marseillaise.*

While no original score of *La Praline* has been located, Jelly Roll Morton played a suite of movements on a recording made for the Library of Congress. Other authorities like Jack Laine were clearly conversant with the composition. A transcription of Morton's piano version was included in Rudi Blesh's Shining Trumpets, making it possible to reconstitute the dance.

Morton claimed to have converted one movement to the last theme of *Tiger Rag* but an alternative account credits this to band leader/trombonist Jack Carey who with Kid Ory was developing the New Orleans tailgate style around 1912 or 1913. His band apparently called it *Play Jack Carey*. Much later the Original Dixieland Jazz Band copyrighted the tune *Tiger Rag* that is clearly based on the movements of the Quadrille that were demonstrated by Morton.

---

110 Charters op cit p41

La Praline included five strains:

> Introduction,
> Waltz,
> Mazurka,
> Polka
> 2/4 Ragtime Dance.

Morton's demonstration also gives us a glimpse of the early manner of performance of Waltz, Polka and Mazurka.[111]

Two witnesses said Bolden played the *Moonwinks Mazurka*.

Moonwinks, a Three-step mazurka, was published in Chicago in 1904 by George Stevens but there is some likelihood that the dance with the same name was older than that.

The dance is still well known in country-dance circles in the US. It is described in a dance website as:

> '*Moonwinks*—Also known as "The Three Step," a traditional slow waltz.... The old dance originally consisted of only the first 8 meas. The second part was added later to make the dance interesting and more meaningful for modern round dancers, and is now standard. Beginners sometimes use only the first part. The pattern was invented to make use of very slow waltz music. Notice that there is no turning waltz. Routine is done 3 times."

The Bush Dance club of Bendigo also refers to *Moonwinks* among a group of dances used there:

> "... (the) Polka Mazurka: Takes its name from the combination of mazurka dances and polka step turns, but has nothing to do with the 2-4 polka musically, except perhaps for an anacrusis which can help in the mazurka bounce. Musically the Polka Mazurka is a Mazurka in 3-4 time with similar tempo and bass vamp to the waltz. The fundamental difference between the waltz and a mazurka is that extra brightness and bounce created by a two-quaver (dotted) and two-crotchet combination to each bar. *Oh My Darling Clementine* is a typical Polka Mazurka. Authorities vary as to whether the empha-

---

111   see Appendix 1

sis (unlike the waltz) is on the 2nd or 3rd beat. Some Mazurkas have an anacrusis as in Clementine and others start on a marked downbeat as in *Moonwinks* or *Little Pussy*.... The tempo for this group is the same as the sequence dance waltzes, 52-54 bars a minute. The exception is for some regional versions in parts of NSW and Qld where there are glides instead of mazurka hops and the slower tempo is that of the Circular Waltz, 48-50 bars a minute."

Other dance sources suggest the mazurka had an even 3/4 rhythm with an accent on the second beat—thus (.—.) but the last step of the three to the measure is a little hop. Baby Dodds said that although the mazurka was in three four time, at the end of every measure it had what he called: "a little accented 'boomp boomp'—two eighth notes before picking up three four again"[112]

It is significant that New Orleans cornetist Charlie Love listed the 'Polka-Mazooka' as one of the dances performed by the Bolden band at their regular dances.

It appears that the name *Moonwinks* may have occult or fairy connotations possibly of Celtic origin, as in the following poem:

> "Been polishing me pipes
> and tuning up me brays,
> For when it is your bedtime
> The Fae will come out to play.
> For ye will not hear us.
> We plays when you are sleeping.
> Quiet as a bed bug,
> in we come a creepin'.
> We fill your dreams with Faery kisses and
> Moonwinks from on high:
> And wishes for a lifetime
> Of happiness and light."

Dr. Bruce Raeburn of The Jazz Archive at New Orleans' Tulane University made a copy of Stevens' *Moonwinks* piano score available to us along with material from an orchestral arrangement by the composer Laurence Dubuclet. This arrangement gives a very clear idea of

---

[112] Interview with Bill Russel published in 1994

how the tune would have been played by a conventional dance band of Bolden's time.

Moonwinks comprises three themes performed in the sequence: AA, BB, A, CC, BB, AA. The score indicates that it should be played in 'Tempo di Mazurka', whatever that means.

The regular Viennese **Waltz** was extremely popular during Bolden's career, so it is surprising that no record exists of a waltz in his repertoire. Similarly the duple time **Schottische** was in demand.

Juventina Rosa's Mexican waltz *Over The Waves* was published in New Orleans in 1891. It is known to have been very popular among bands of the time, as it is today. It has been included in the repertoire to represent this neglected style.

Similarly, I have included Walter Armstrong's popular sentimental song *Sweet Adeline* of 1903 that can be used to accompany the Schottische.

The dance evening would not be complete without the **Slow March** that accompanied the dancers to the supper table. Charlie Love listed the *Gettysburg March* in his programme but this was not published until 1911. I have included instead Porter Steele's march *(In) High Society* published in 1901. There is evidence that this march, played slow, was still being used for this purpose as late as 1913 and it is known that it was played by Bolden rivals early in the century.

Classical Rags

Some witnesses insisted that Bolden played some of the Classical Piano Rags. These included:

> *Bowery Buck* (Turpin)
> *Frog Legs Rag* (Scott)
> *Maple Leaf Rag* (Joplin)
> *Palm Leaf Rag* (Joplin)
> *Panama Rag* (Seymour)

<u>*Bowery Buck*</u> by Tom Turpin was published in 1899—advertised as "The most original "Rag-time" piece ever written. It is generally considered to be a survival of the earlier folk ragtime style and contains 'buck and wing figures' in the second theme. It is believed it was composed following a trip to New York and may have been partly based on a tune Turpin heard being played by an organ

grinder on the street. Bunk Johnson, who said it was played by the Bolden band referred to it as *Brewery Buck*.

Frog Legs Rag (1906) written by James Scott is a much more complex rag. It comprises four intricate themes and an interlude (or Bridge) in the form AA BB A Interlude CC DD. An arrangement by Scott Joplin, for band instruments in A major, was published in the so called Red Backed Book of Rags by Joplin's publisher John Stark around 1912, too late to have been used by the Bolden band, though later New Orleans bands used it.

The Maple Leaf Rag by Scott Joplin was the rag that made his name when published in 1899. Some witnesses doubted that Bolden played it, though others insist he did. Like *Frog Legs Rag* it has four themes in a typical ragtime form—AA BB A CC DD. Sydney Bechet said the less talented bands memorised the themes and played their own 'head arrangements' of the *Maple Leaf Rag*.

Palm Leaf Rag (1903) by Joplin is a Slow Drag and the piano score carries the injunction—"Play a little slow". It has an Introduction and four rather beautiful flowing themes in the pattern—Introduction AA BB CC DD. Though Joplin played the slow drag at a medium slow tempo it seems the New Orleans bands may have played it even more slowly.

Panama Rag was composed by C.Seymour and published in 1904. It is a March tempo rag in 2/4 time in the pattern—Introduction AA BB CC DD. The inclusion of this rag in Bolden's repertoire should not be confused with the 1911 tango style composition *Panama* by W.H Tyers that forms part of the standard repertoire of many later bands.

As indicated above some authorities have suggested that Bolden was not skilled enough to play the more complex rags like *Maple Leaf Rag*, and Charlie Love said that they only played one or two of "Those Old Rags" an evening.

Popular Song and Popular Theatre

Readers accustomed to the regular repertoire of traditional jazz may find the inclusion of 'old fashioned' popular songs in Bolden's repertoire puzzling. However there is strong evidence of a movement towards black participation in the popular theatre of the time.[113] Many of the popular songs at the beginning of the 1890's contained musical influences from earlier black popular culture albeit they still pandered to white sensibilities by continuing to portray blacks in caricature. Black audiences were increasingly able to attend the theatre and watch black artists like the soprano Sissieretta Jones performing. It is not surprising that black audiences of Bolden's time adapted to the time and called for popular songs that originated in stage shows to be included in the dance repertoire.

---

113 see Morgan and Barlow op cit p21 and Abbot and Seroff op cit Chapters 3 and 4

Chapter 5

The Repertoire Part 2
Black Vernacular Songs and Blues

"He played nothing but blues and all that stink music, and he played it loud."

—Pops Foster

The inclusion of so many vernacular dance songs in the repertoire illustrates what was happening in the transition from conventional 19th century dance music to Elemental Jazz. The unconventional music of the streets and beer halls was penetrating the dance halls.

The Dance Songs and Blues

The dance songs and blues were genuine survivals of an earlier stream of vernacular music that had been developing from slave music since Emancipation. They were easily played in the emerging syncopated and improvised manner. Vulgar, and often pornographic, words and titles abound in the list. Some of them can be tracked to earlier sources. Others seem to have appeared around Bolden's time, and some were believed by old musicians to have been composed by him. I was unable to find an original score for any of them, though later versions of melody and/or lyrics abound in published fake books and on the Internet, sometimes purporting to have been composed by folk or jazz musicians of a later period. Some of them have been recorded many times by traditional bands and folk singers.

Fast Dance Songs

Four of the dance songs are lively airs well suited to dancing the ragtime two-step:

All the Whores Like the Way I Ride
Get Out of Here (Go on Home)
If You Don't Shake (You Get No Cake)
Makin' Runs

In Bolden's time they would likely have been called **jump ups, reels** or **ditties**.

Fig.13 Above: A white artist's impression of dancing to a fiddle in a bar or barrelhouse. Maybe it was a jig or cakewalk.

Sam Charters described the tune of *If You Don't Shake* as:

"... an instrumental melodic line, disjunct, harmonically organized, and in a standard dance rhythm with simple syncopation."[114]

---

114 Charters op cit p15

This describes each of them well. They are, if you like, prototypes from which later jazz stomps were derived.

Information is sparse about *All the Whores Like the Way I Ride*, though Wooden Joe Nicholas, a Bolden disciple, and Bunk Johnson made recordings of the song in the 1940's.

Similarly, there is little information about the derivation of *Get Out of Here*, though witnesses said Bolden played it at the end of the rougher dances instead of *Home Sweet Home*. Chorus and verse were more recently published under the names of Kid Ory and Bud Scott. (1961)

If You Don't Shake has been described as Bolden's theme song, and some witnesses thought it was a Bolden original. According to Charters:

> "Bolden's theme song was remembered by several musicians as IF YOU DON'T SHAKE or P.I., a Storyville term for pimp."

It appears to have had two themes, the first a lively cakewalk dance that Charters transcribed and published, and the second, a cakewalk march tune sometimes called *"I May Be Crazy but I Ain't No Fool"*. These themes were demonstrated in an archival recording by Jelly Roll Morton that has particularly salacious words.[115] The second theme also turned up in the 1906 ragtime composition *Dixie Queen* by Robert Hoffman accompanied by another theme (*Ti-na-na*), that also appears along with both of the *If You Don't Shake* themes in an orchestral recording by Jelly Roll Morton of 1940 (*Mama's Got a Baby*). Interestingly, the first theme of *If You Don't Shake* and the *Ti-na-na* theme are very similar.

Gushee found evidence that the 'Te-na-na' (sic) was a dance popular with lower class dance audiences in New Orleans in 1911.[116] Witnesses said the Bolden band played *If You Don't Shake* for street parades.

Makin' Runs is another lively ditty of a cakewalk character, that appeared in an interview with Bunk Johnson recorded around 1940. Johnson whistled it as a demonstration of the way he thought Buddy

---

115 Circle 1684b and Rounder CD 1094
"If you don't shake, don't get no cake,
If you don't rock, don't get no cock.
I said, if you don't shake, don't get no cake,
If you don't rock, you don't get no cock.
If you don't fuck, you don't have no luck,
(laughs)

116 Gushee BMRJ p20

Bolden played, and later recorded variations on the tune with a piano accompaniment as a demonstration of Bolden's style.

I was fortunate in obtaining a transcription of the whistled version from a Swedish ragtime enthusiast. If Johnson is correct, this may be the closest we can get to the sound of the Bolden band. Johnson said it was just a tune Bolden made up. He pointed out the 'breaks" in the tune which he said were of those played in the Bolden band, typically by valve trombonist Willie Cornish. There have been attempts to find a source for the melody in earlier published sources, none of which are very persuasive.[117]

Folk Songs

Three of the dance songs have old folk roots. Presumably they could have been heard on street corners, or on the riverbank levees:

1. *Funky Butt* is the most famous tune played by Bolden. Jelly Roll Morton thought Buddy composed tune but actually it is a very old folk song (at least as old as the 1860's). In Buddy's time it might have been called *'Doin' the Ping Pong'*.
   The *Funky Butt* name was acquired in Kinney's Hall ca 1900. It was a hot night and the hall was poorly ventilated; the dancing crowd was sweating, and the atmosphere became foul. Trombonist Will Cornish improvised and sang new words about the smell.
   The song became known ever after as *'Funky Butt'* and the hall the Funky Butt Hall.
   Jelly Roll Morton made several recordings of the song under the title of *Buddy Bolden's Blues* but several authorities including Sydney Bechet expressed the opinion that the Morton's ensemble version was too slow. It also appears too nostalgic. However in view of evidence that Bolden's Band did not play very fast numbers a moderate blues tempo suitable for dancing appears appropriate. Possibly the band was playing for dancers doing the Ping Pong. Unfortunately we do not know much about the dance.

---

117 *Happy Sammy—a Teasin Rag* (1906) by F.C.Schmidt and the Mexican march *Zacatecas* have been suggested. Examination of these scores reveals only remote resemblances to *Makin' Runs*.

Louis James' String Band made a recording under the title *King Bolden's Song* with the main theme containing fewer of the characteristics of Morton's personal style.

It seems clear that the band members sang the chorus, possibly together. A New Orleans journalist writing in the 1930's wrote that the real words were unprintable. Bearing in mind the meaning of the title, the following, compiled from various sources including Lorenzo Staultz (Bolden's second guitar player) would appear authentic:

> "I thought I heard Buddy Bolden say:
> Funky Butt, Funky Butt;
> Take it away!
> I thought I heard Buddy Bolden say:
> Nasty Butt, Stinkin' Gut;
> Take it away!
> And let Mr. Bolden play".

Alternatively the third line could be varied to "Dirty nasty stinkin' butt take it away"

As indicated above, Morton thought that the melody, an original Bolden composition, was later stolen by the authors of a rag called the *St. Louis Tickle* published in 1904. (The theme also appeared in ragtime composer Ben Harney's C*akewalk in the Sky* published in 1899.) However there are traces of it going back to the Civil War, probably having been carried to New Orleans by upriver boatmen:

> "I thought I heer'd Mr. Lincoln shout,
> Rebels close down them plantations
> and let all them niggers out.
> I'm positive I heer'd Mr Lincoln shout,
> Rebels close them plantations
> and let all them niggers out,
> You gonna lose this war, git on your knees and pray,
> That's the words I heer'd Mr Lincoln say."[118]

Here Bolden was "tapping into a developing blues tradition that was emerging from earlier vernacular shout based practices."[119]

---

118 Marquis 1978/1993 p 110
119 Extract from "The Ancestry of Jazz: A Musical Family History" D. Hardie 2004

1. *My Bucket's Got a Hole In It* is a very old song clearly of folk origins—still popular with folk singers and Traditional jazz bands alike. We have to imagine it originally being performed in a New Orleans beer hall or countryside Juke house, perhaps with some audience participation.

    It has a very simple melody and a number of varying lyrics have been recorded. We don't know just which words Bolden used so I found it necessary to adapt score and lyrics from numerous folk sources that appear authentic. It is probably related to another folk song *"Dear Lisa—There's a Hole in the Bucket"*. It was played around 1900 by Bolden's Band and after 1906 by Frank Duson's Eagle Band. It was said Bolden played it "when he spotted friends or some of the sporting crowd and he wanted to liven things up." Lorenzo Staultz who played guitar with both bands apparently sang it with wine spilling from his mouth.

2. *The Old Cow Died and Old Brock Cried* is another folk melody Bolden adapted for his own purposes.[120] He apparently composed a parody on the famous folk song *"The Tune The Old Cow Died On"*:

VERSE 1
In from th' field came farmer Brown, Friday aternoon
He sat down 'neath th' Maple tree
An' sang himself a tune
He sang till th' cows came running home
Around him formed a ring
For never before since th' world was made
Had th' farmer tried t' sing
An' this is th song tri-fa-da-da
Da song 'neath th' Maple tree
Tri-fa-da-da-tri-fa-da-da-da
It's th' tune th' old cow died on

VERSE 2
The oldest cow in th' farmers herd
She tried t' sing this song
She tried so hard but she could not sing
Tho her voice was loud an' strong

---

120 Marquis op cit p108

>   Th' farmer laughed, th' tears rolled down
>   His cheeks like apples red
>   But th' cow kept trying t' sing this song
>   Till at last she fell down dead
>   Now this is th' tune tri-fa-da-da
>   Da song 'neath th' Maple tree
>   Tri-fa-da-da-tri-fa-da-da-da
>   It's th' tune th' old cow died on etc.

We can only speculate on the exact words sung by the whole Bolden band in what was a joke aimed at their guitarist Jefferson 'Brock' Mumford.

Sydney Bechet said that the tune they used was similar to *Muskat Ramble*[121] and at least one folk singer recorded a version with a tune somewhat like the first theme of Kid Ory's composition. I also found another folk tune that is a variation on the theme.

Blues

Ragtime, jazz and the blues appeared about the same time, though the blues did not become widely known until the first published blues appeared in 1911. The blues is generally believed to have evolved from the work shouts sung by cotton workers and corn farmers in the years after Emancipation. Buddy Bolden is considered to have been the inventor of the 'hot' instrumental blues. As with the other items in the repertoire he seems to have gathered them from a variety of sources.

Five blues compositions appear in the list:

> *Careless Love*
> *If You Don't Like My Potatoes why do you Dig So Deep?*
> *Make Me a Pallet On the Floor*
> *Mamie's Blues (2/19 Blues)*
> *Salty Dog*

1. <u>*Careless Love*</u>
    Buddy Bolden was regarded by his New Orleans contemporaries as the first to introduce the blues to dance music. They

---

[121] Believed to have been be composed By Kid Ory

mentioned *"Careless Love"* as one of the blues he regularly played and some even thought he had composed the tune.

However, *"Careless Love"* was a very old mountain folk song found by folk song collectors in many US states. John and Alan Lomax thought that it was one of the earliest blues, probably of white origin, and perhaps even the first of all blues. It had appeared before 1900. Much later, in 1925, W.C.Handy published a version of *Careless Love* and it became a popular favourite of blues singers.

Bolden's biographer Don Marquis found an old lady who said Buddy composed his own words to the tune:

> "Ain't it hard to love another woman's man
> Ain't it hard to love another woman's man
> You can't get him when you want him
> You have to catch him when you can."[122]

There are numerous variants of the main tune from folk sources, ranging from a simple version published by the Lomaxes to the two-theme Handy publication.

Apparently the early New Orleans bands preceded the chorus of *Careless Love* with a twelve bar blues and later recordings by Bolden contemporaries Wooden Joe Nicholas and Oscar Celestin illustrate this.

2. *If You Don't Like My Potatoes Why Do You Dig So Deep?* This is one of a number of vulgar blues listed by Guitarist Danny Barker as songs Bolden introduced late in the evening as the sporty crowd began to arrive. I have only been able to find two of them. Fortunately, two recordings were made of the blues in the 1920's so it is possible to recreate the melody and words.

3. *Get Your Big Leg Off of Me* is the second of these vulgar blues. H.J.Boiusseaux, a white pianist who had worked in New Orleans sporting houses, recorded a version that has three themes that we were able to transcribe. It had no words. It is similar, but not identical with *Big Fat Woman Blues*. A number of versions of the latter have been recorded, including one by Huddy Leadbetter. The words vary from version to version, but the following is typical:

---

122 Marquis D. op cit p107

> Hey big mama
> Hey big mama
> Callin' hey big mama
> Take your big legs off of me
> Lovin' you mama gonna be killin' me
> Lovin' big fat mama gonna be killin' me
> Hey hey mama get your big legs off of me

4. *Make Me a Pallet on the Floor.*
This is widely recognised as having been a favourite of Bolden's audience. George Baquet heard it played on the occasion when he was invited to play with the band:

> "Buddy held up his cornet, paused to be sure of his embouchure, then they played *Make me a Pallet on the Floor*. Everybody got up quick, the whole place rose and yelled out, 'Oh, Mr. Bolden, play it for us, Buddy, play it!'"[123]

The melody line appears in various forms in numerous folk song collections, with various words sung by white and black folk performers.
When asked to demonstrate Buddy Bolden's style on record Bunk Johnson played a number of variations on *Make Me a Pallet*.
It is difficult to say what dance was performed to this blues. Baby Dodds said:

> "The very lowest type of dancers used to love such things. They were played very slow and fellows and their girl friends would stand almost still and just make movements ... we played the blues in a very slow tempo. Blues today (1959) aren't played as slow as in the old days ..."[124]

This blues appears to have been widely known outside New Orleans. Jelly Roll Morton said it was known in New Orleans before he was born (i.e. before 1890). It appeared also in the Blind Boone medley of *'Southern Rags'* published in 1908, sug-

---

123 Shapiro and Hentoff op cit p38
124 The Baby Dodds story 1959 p29

gesting that it may have been one of the vernacular songs regularly played by the folk ragtime piano players in the pre-ragtime era.

This appears to confirm the view that Buddy was among the first to incorporate the emerging blues into his performances, just at the time when the blues was becoming a recognised form.

Jelly Roll Morton stated that there were great blues players in the Storyville houses around 1901 and 1902 that "didn't know nothing but the blues" and he demonstrated examples of blues they played, including *Make Me a Pallet on the Floor*. He demonstrated the song, including his own extremely pornographic words.[125] Bolden too appears to have had his own words to *Make me a Pallet on the Floor*:

> "Make me a pallet on the floor,
> Make me a pallet on the floor,
> Make it soft make it low.
> So your sweet man will never know."[126]

5. *Mamie's Blues (2/19 Blues)*

Jelly Roll Morton introduced Mamie's Blues like this:

> "There happened to be a woman, that lived next door to my godmother's, in the Garden District. Her name was Mamie Desdoume[127]. On her right hand, she had her two middle fingers between her forefingers cut off, and she played with the three. So she played a … a blues like this. All day long when she first would get up in the morning. She used to sing for us like this:

> 'I stood on the corner, my feet was dripping wet,
> Stood on the corner, my feet was dripping wet,
> I asked every man I met.
> Can't give me a dollar, give me a lousy dime,
> You can't give me a dollar, give me a lousy dime,
> Just to feed that hungry man of mine.

---

125 Lomax 1952 and Rounder CD 1092
126 Extract from Hardie D. "The Ancestry of Jazz"
127 Recent research suggests that what Morton actually said was Mamie Desdunes but this has been transcribed incorrectly as Desdoume.

> I've got a husband, and I've got a kid man too,
> I've got a husband, I've got a kid man too,
> My husband can't do what my ... kid man can do.
> I like the way he cooks my cabbage for me,
> I like the way he cooks my cabbage for me,
> Looks like he sets my natural soul free.'

Morton said this was the first blues he ever heard, and it is believed it formed part of Bolden's regular repertoire.

6. <u>Salty Dog</u> is a very well known blues, usually attributed to Papa Charlie Jackson who recorded it with Fred Keppard's Jazz Cardinals. It is a very old blues still sung by folk singers who sing differing versions of the words. Papa Charlie Jackson sang:

> 'Never had no one woman at a time
> Always had six seven eight or nine
> Salty Dog
> Oh! You Salty Dog
> God made the women (sic)
> He made her mighty funny
> Kiss em in the lips
> Sweet as any honey
> Salty Dog
> You Salty Dog'

Spirituals

Buddy Bolden's regular attendance at the First St Baptist Church brought him into contact with a stream of black religious music that had antecedents in the nationwide religious revivals of the 1840's. Congregations of this kind sang Jubilee songs and spirituals descended from the earlier holy songs or ring shouts. By Buddy's time many of these songs had been published and promoted worldwide in a tradition of concert spirituals. Contemporary witnesses alleged Bolden only went to church to get music for his band.

There are three spirituals included in the list:

Go Down Moses
Ride On King Jesus
Run Mary (Strumpet) Run

Some other hymns have been suggested but their association with Bolden is not certain.

1. <u>Go Down Moses</u> is probably the earliest published spiritual, being published in 1867 as *The Song of the Contrabands*, but it is older than that. The contrabands were slaves who escaped from their owners during the civil war and sought asylum with Union forces at Fort Monroe in South Eastern Virginia. It was first heard, and taken down, by the Chaplain to the contrabands who considered it had been sung among the escapees for some time before their escape. I found a number of scores, including one in four part harmonies published in a history of the Fisk Jubilee Singers around 1886:

   > When Israel was in Egypt's Land
   > Let my people go!
   > Oppressed so hard they could not stand
   > Let my people go!
   > Go down Moses
   > Way down In Egypt's land
   > Tell ole Pharaoh,
   > Let my people go!

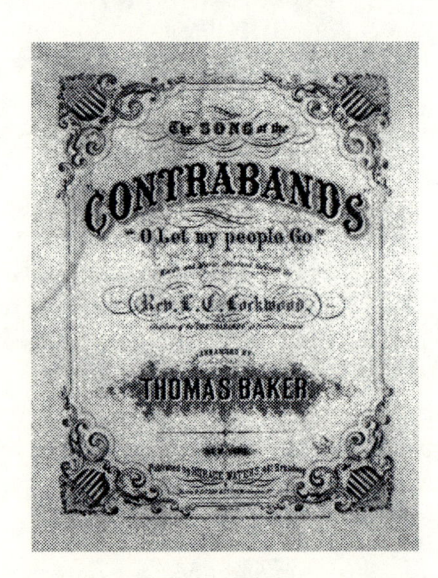

Fig.14 Above: Sheet Music Cover of *Go Down Moses* published as *The Song of the Contrabands* in 1867

2. <u>Ride on King (Jesus)</u> was published in a book of American slave songs in 1867[128] but it also is probably older than that. From 1870 it, too, formed part of the repertoire of the Fisk Jubilee Singers who introduced Negro Spirituals to the popular media after 1870.

> "Ride on King Jesus; No man can hinder Him,
> Ride on King Jesus; No man can hinder Him
> King Jesus rides on a milk white horse,
> No man can hinder him,
> The river of Jordan He did cross
> No man can hinder him."

Other versions, possibly older, are entitled *No Man Can Hinder Me*. I found another set of words with Civil War overtones, entitled *Ride In Kind Saviour* that reads:

> "Ride in kind Saviour!
> No man can hinder me.
> O, Jesus is a mighty man!
> No man can hinder me &c.
> We're Marchin through Virginny field.
> No man, &c.
> O, Satan is a busy mans,
> No man, &c.
> And he has his sword and shield,
> No man, &c.
> O, old Secesh done come and gone!
> No man can hinder me."

Some witnesses have suggested that Bolden would have altered the words for secular performance, possibly with vulgar connotations. No record survives of the adapted words of *Ride on King Jesus* but the word Jesus seems to have dropped out of the title. Zue Robertson described hearing a performance of *Ride On King* during which Bolden blew so hard he blew the tuning slide out of his cornet!!

3. <u>Run Mary (Nigger) Run</u> While there was no difficulty finding the above spirituals. *Run Mary Run* presented problems. There are

---

128 Allen W.F. Ware C.P. W. McKim-Garrison Lucy "Slave Songs of the United States", 1867

numerous early variants of the folk reels *Run Nigger Run, Run Mary Run* and *Run Sinner Run* to be found, but it is not clear which would have been the one used by Bolden. The most persuasive one is:

> 'O some tell me that a Nigger won't steal,
> But I've seen a Nigger in my cornfield;
> O run, nigger, run, for the pateroller will catch you
> O run Nigger Run, for tis almost day'

This appears to be a later variant of the pre Emancipation *Run Mary Run*. Bolden is believed to have altered the words of *Run Mary Run* to *Run Strumpet Run*.

Sam Charters suggested that Bolden took the harmonies from tunes in Baptist hymnbooks and taught them to his band. There is no supporting evidence for that, but the version of *Ride On King Jesus* from an early book of Southern folk songs is in 4-part harmony, giving the option to explore that approach.

As the melody is often constructed in the form of a call and response between leader and congregation it also allows us to explore the musical opportunities for alternating responses and breaks. Even today trombonists often play along with the congregational singing in Baptist churches.

A contemporary said that Buddy made the cornet 'moan like a Baptist preacher'—introducing blue notes.

Above all, the rhythmic structure of these spirituals features the exaggerated after beat emphasis derived from the Jubilee singing, hand clapping and heel tapping that probably led to jazz rhythm.

The Revised Repertoire

A number of tunes had to be left out of the list, either because no score or recording could be found, or because actual publication dates suggested an attribution that, like that of the *Gettysburg March*, appeared anachronistic. A number of others which witnesses said, "everybody played" were also omitted.

So there we have it, a catalogue of tunes you might have heard uptown in the Masonic Hall in 1903. It is a mixture of popular 'coon' and sentimental songs; folk songs, raunchy ditties and blues; modified spirituals and piano rags along with conventional dance compositions; a mixture representative of the musical tastes of an audience apparently equally at home with the outpourings of the sophisticated nationwide publishing industry and with surviving songs from of the black vernacular folk and religious traditions.

But what did it sound like?

Chapter 6

How They Played

"Of course. I remember. It was only a year or two back, when I was house cleaning. They looked like old Dictaphone records. They were old and just sitting there, collecting dust. They went to the dump."
"One of them was the first jazz record," I said, but I was talking to myself.[129]

In 1939 the record collector/historian Charles Edward Smith interviewed Willie Cornish who had played valve trombone in the Bolden Orchestra before 1900. He wrote that Cornish told him "more than anyone could have bargained for about the style and repertoire of the Bolden band." This information was turned over to the writers of the ground breaking jazz history book Jazzmen that appeared in that year. Smith had heard that the Bolden band could have made a wax cylinder recording before 1898, and conducted an extensive search for the cylinder. Cornish told him the recording was made at the suggestion of one of Cornish's friends. Smith pressed Cornish:

> '"You're sure about that cylinder aren't you?" He replied patiently that he should be, he'd helped make it and he had heard it many times;'[130]

Smith continued his search but no trace of the recording has since been found.

---

129 C, E, Smith "The Bolden Cylinder' Saturday Review March 16 1957
130 C, E, Smith "The Bolden Cylinder' Saturday Review March 16 1957

However Smith also pointed out that in 1939 there were musicians alive that had played with Bolden, or with other first generation bands and others who had heard him many times—and even descriptions of Bolden's personal style. They fall into two groups: accounts by players old enough to have played between 1896 and 1906; and those of younger musicians who were old enough to have heard the bands of that time.

Fig.15 Above: Bolden Band members Willie Cornish (Valve Trombone) and Willie Warner (Clarinet).

Willie Cornish's description of how the Bolden Band played was apparently subsumed in the chapters of *Jazzmen*, but there other accounts of early jazz performance that can give us an idea of how the music was performed and sounded.

There is evidence that the musical style did not suddenly change after 1906 and that it was played in much the same fashion until around 1912 at the height of the ragtime craze, when some instrumental changes occurred and classical rags and march tunes began to be played in a more vigorous manner. Consequently information from players active in the later period that confirms earlier descriptions can also be taken seriously.

What they said

Here is what some of them had to say:[131]

---

[131] The summary has been drawn from many sources. Detailed references can be found in the various chapters of the Author's previous works; "The Loudest Trumpet Buddy Bolden and the Early History of Jazz" and "Exploring Early Jazz—the Origins and Evolution of the New Orleans Style".

Wallace Collins who played with Bolden
"At the beginning Bolden had cornet, clarinet, (valve) trombone, violin, guitar, bass violin, traps

... the violin played straight melody, Bolden ragged the melody except on loud passages. The introduction they bust out loud as they can.

... to rag the melody Bolden would take a note and put two or three to it."

Albert Glenny who played with Bolden.
"(Bolden) ... had a right good tone, too, and a lively style. With all those notes he'd throw in and out of nowhere, You never heard anything like it."

Jelly Roll Morton
".... The composer (of Funky Butt) ... was Buddy Bolden. The most powerful ... trumpet player I've ever heard ... or ever was known.

... I used to go out to *Lincoln Park* myself when Buddy Bolden was out there. Because I used to like to hear him play an'outblow everybody.

... He was the blowingest man that ever lived since Gabriel.

Peter Bocage
..."(Bolden) had a good tone, didn't know what he was doing, didn't read. He played everything in B flat. He played a lot of blues, slow drag, not too many fast numbers. Those fellows played B flat, E flat or F sharp (??), but get three or four flats or three or four sharps and they was out of it. Blues was their standby, slow blues. They played mostly medium tempo."

Pops Foster:
"The (violinist) called the numbers, stomped off and played the violin as the lead instrument.

... The fiddler could read and taught the rest of the band the numbers and played a whole lot of everything.

... In the early days when you had a solo the other instruments were always doing something behind the solo. None of the guys took their horns down for a chorus to let another guy play a solo.
... The bands that couldn't read could play nothing but choruses. They'd play nothing but chorus after chorus.
... Bolden was just a chorus man.... Most of the New Orleans bands of the day, you didn't hear them play a full number.... They never did make no coda, they'd end on the coda and make their own ending."

John St Cyr:
"... The violin would play ensemble and every strain—playing softly when featuring the clarinet in low register.
... the violin was also lead instrument with the cornet and would trade off and the cornet player would take down to save his lip
... the clarinet would play obbligato, second or side melody
... the trombone played third or bass part, no slide effects
... brass instruments did not play as loud as they do in these days (1960)
... the bass hit 1 and 3 with little runs for two or four measures ... the guitar hit straight four beats with little runs to break up the monotony ... The Bass drum played straight one and three beats." (*He said that drummers had their individual jazzy styles on the snare drum.*)
(Of Keppard's time ca 1906/1912): "Bands as a whole still played ensemble style. On certain numbers they would feature the cornet player, another number would feature the trombone player. Clarinet was always featured. (The clarinet style) was "about the same as today"
"... most of them could spell ... playing hot came after we had learned the number—a head arrangement.
In the 'hot' or last chorus everyone in the band cut loose, including the bass ... the bass is entitled to play 4 beats to the measure in the last chorus."

Danny Barker:
"They used a fiddle player to play the lead—a fiddle player could read—and that was to give them some protection ... Buddy Bolden would say, 'Simmer down, let me hear the sound of them feet.' ... they'd shade the music ... The rhythm then often would play that mixture of African and Spanish rhythm."

Bebe Ridgely:
"... It would sound a little different from today's (1961) bands with the double beat which is fast four four time ... The Bolden Band played a slower two beat ... the trombone part was fundamentally a bass part but sometimes filled in open spots, played harmony with another horn and sometimes took the lead."

Bill Matthews
"... and on those old slow blues, that boy could make them women jump out of the window. On those old, slow, low down blues, he had a moan in his cornet that went right through you, just like you were in church or something ... He was the sweetest trumpet player in the world.... Louis Armstrong, King Oliver, none of them had a tone like Bolden."[132] ... "He found those things to put in a blues, like old levee camps and like that, maken a spiritual feeling go through you. He had a cup, a specially made cup that made that cornet moan like a Baptist preacher"[133]

Bunk Johnson:
"... Now here is the thing that made King Bolden's band the first band to play jazz. It was because they couldn't read at all.... Bolden played pretty much by ear. And made up his own tunes."

"... I can give you an idea of it (*Bolden's Style*) by whistling one of Buddy's old tunes ... the runs that Cornish would make, what you call solos today, Buddy Bolden

---

132 Marquis op cit p 100
133 HJA 1959

and Cornish would call them runs. They'd make a dead break, and the trombone would make it …"
He whistled a series of 5 variations on the tune we call 'Makin Runs'. (2 in Bb, 3 in Eb). Hearing the recording later he said "That's Bolden to a T" and pointed out the breaks that he said were Cornish's. He said it had no title "No just a make up chorus of Buddy's."

<u>Gunther Schuller:</u>
(Reviewing Bunk Johnson's' demonstrations of Bolden style)
"… Bunk's demonstration … reminds us that this style did not permit improvisation in the strictest sense of that term. It consisted more of embellishment of a melody than improvisation on chords, and much outright repetition. Here of course we have the crucial difference between New Orleans and other styles." *(He then mentions Louis Armstrong creating a new chord based style of improvisation during his Chicago days.)*

By 1900 there were at least nine or ten bands playing the new syncopated dance music. The early improvising bands were performing a transitional type of music, taking the regular dance music of the New Orleans dance halls, and converting it to what was later to be known as jazz.

It can be seen from the above that a consistent performance style had emerged. There was a short period of experimentation with instrumentation. One band, for example, had a piccolo lead instead of the violin, and Bolden tried a second clarinet as leader. However the most common pattern seems to have been to have a violinist leader.

Ensemble Improvisation

Their regular practice was to emphasise the melody which was carried at all times, usually by the violinist.

The violinist beat in the time and led the performance as was normal in the traditional dance orchestra setting. One witness said that in the first chorus they all played the melody straight.

Thereafter the individual members improvised paraphrases on the melody, ragging the tune by varying the duration and emphasis of individual cadences in an informal raggy manner, called by some musicologists *heterephony*. (This was to become a looser Free Ragtime in the next decade.) There were no whole chorus solos, so, to provide variety, the melody line was passed around, with one instrument restating the melody in the foreground while others ragged behind the lead. (The violin continued to restate the melody throughout.)

Breaks and trombone bass runs were also introduced to provide variety, as had been done in the earlier brass band compositions.

Variety was further provided by variation in volume. Bolden's band played very loudly but on some choruses the volume was dropped to allow the rhythm to come through. This created an elementary swing. In the blues the Spanish habanera beat was sometimes introduced in such choruses.

Tempo was not as fast as that of jazz bands recorded after 1917, and rhythm was suited to the dance steps of the time, eg. Waltz, Two-step and Slow drag.

Some were known as Chorus bands, that is they didn't play the verses and codas of popular songs, only the choruses, but sometimes composed their own endings. This group may have included Buddy Bolden's band and it's successor Frank Duson's Eagle Band. They were said to play mainly in Bb, but sometimes in F and Eb.

The bands also sang extempore vocal choruses to add variety. The best known of these were Bolden's *Funky Butt* and *Old Brock Cried When The Old Cow Died*.

'Variating' the Tune

New Orleans Jazz writer Bill Russel called the essential characteristic of the New Orleans Style 'variating the tune'. From the above analysis it is possible to define the essential elements of the Elemental Jazz Performance Style:

- **Heterophony:**[134] The melody was kept going. In fact the melody was passed around among the horn players accompanied by the whole band playing melody, harmony or 'noodling around'.

---

134 'Simultaneous individual elaborations of the melody'.

Bunk Johnson said that the only solos played were breaks inserted into the melody and these were called 'runs'.

- **Paraphrase improvisation:** Gunther Schuller described it as "more an embellishment of the melody than variation on the chords".
- **Raggin' the tune:** "taking the melody and varying the notes by shortening or lengthening them or anticipating the next measure by a half beat. Early witnesses also talked of doubling or tripling the notes" (eg. Substituting two quavers for a crotchet.)
- **Blues Intonation:** Inserting blue notes, smears, and other sounds into the performance.

Within this general framework individual bands developed their individual styles. As we have seen above, some played the chorus of a tune but not the verse, didn't play any introductions or codas but sometimes made up their own endings. Some worked out simple routines they memorised. They were called "routineers" by more skilled musicians. A restricted range of keys was sometimes used (Bb, Eb and F) and witnesses said that tunes were not played as fast as later became common. Bands and individuals played loud but varied volume or rhythm for variety.

Ragging

An essential feature of Elemental Jazz was the adoption from the black vernacular of the practice known as **raggin'**, not to be confused with ragtime.

C.E. Smith pointed out that early jazzmen had:

> "… borrowed a word from up the river—causing a lot of confusion amongst jazz historians later on by calling themselves ragtime bands."[135]

Ragging can be traced back to pre Emancipation Afro-American music[136] and it is clearly one of the influences that led to ragtime.

---
135 CE Smith "The Bolden Cylinder" The Saturday Review March 16 1957
136 see Hardie D. "The Ancestry of Jazz—A Musical Family History" Chapter 14 p174ff

Ragtime largely depends for its syncopation on repeated three-note syncopated figures previously absorbed into American popular music from African and Latin sources.

[Musical notation: Ex.1 — Folk song melody / Piano rag version / Ragtime bass]

Ex.1 Example of ragging from Blind Boone's ragtime adaptation of the folk blues *Make Me a Pallet on the Floor*.
Note the typical 'untied ragtime syncopations', consisting of quaver, crotchet and quaver at end of first and third measures.

However as we a have seen above, Bolden and his contemporaries threw in syncopations *as they went along,* by doubling notes (replacing one note by two notes half as long) or extending a note, say, by half it's length.

Willie Cornish said:

> "the Bolden band changed the notes and time values ..."
> and "When we got going they'd cross three tunes[137] at once ..."

It is this ad-lib syncopation by ragging that distinguishes early jazz from written ragtime. Bunk Johnson's demonstration of Bolden's style mentioned above contains many examples of the use of such doubling of notes. Once the leader had mastered the tune each individual member was free to develop his own variations within the context of the head arrangement that stipulated how the various themes and breaks were to be put together.

---

137 Originally quoted in *Jazzmen* as <u>three times</u> at once but Collins said that Bill Russel assured him that Cornish actually said <u>three tunes</u> at once. See Collins op cit p22

Memphis Musician Buster Bailey described what he had heard during an early visit to New Orleans:

> "At that time I wouldn't have known what they meant by improvisation, but embellishment was a phrase I understood. And that was what they were doing in New Orleans—embellishment."[138]

---

138 Shapiro and Hentoff op cit p77

Chapter 7

Reconstructing Elemental Jazz

"The anonymous pioneers presumably Negro for the most part, who gave impetus to the Americanisation process remain silvery shadows on daguerreotypes that have yielded their image to time. They are of a period of popular music and popular dance that deserves the sort of contemplative study that would go beyond research to imaginative reconstruction based upon archaeological analogy".[139]

In previous works I have suggested that there is sufficient information available to permit a more or less faithful recreation of the sounds of early jazz, provided that the approach successfully pioneered by the early music specialists to the works of classical composers is employed.[140] This involved applying the results of research into instrumentation and performance practices based on descriptive texts, letters, reviews, contemporary drawings, teaching manuals and original scores.

I had discussed this idea with a number of correspondents in 2003 in the hope of encouraging others to take on the project. I was at that time fully occupied completing the *Ancestry of Jazz—A Musical Family History*.

However with the publication of that book in early 2004 I began to turn my thoughts to the possibility of starting a recreation project with

---

139 Wilder A. "American Popular Song" OUP NY 1972 Introduction
140 Hardie D "The Loudest Trumpet Buddy Bolden and the Early History of Jazz" Chapter 12 and "Exploring Early Jazz—The Origins and Evolution of the New Orleans Style" Chapter 11

local musicians. I mentioned the idea to an old friend Trevor Rippingale, leader of the New Wolverines Jazz Orchestra, one day over lunch. His response was enthusiastic. He offered to assist with getting the idea off the ground. This was fortunate because, though I had been deeply involved in the local jazz scene in the past, my own contact with the present day musicians was practically non-existent. Trevor on the other hand had an extensive network of musical associates.

He began discussing the concept with colleagues and found some were attracted to the idea. Although they did not have much of an appreciation of music of the Bolden era they were intrigued. After discussion we agreed that we should approach Geoff Bull trumpeter-leader of the Olympia Jazz Band to seek his support. Geoff is one of Australia's leading New Orleans stylists, and he has had extensive experience performing with bands in New Orleans and elsewhere. He has also accumulated a wealth of historical knowledge about early jazz.

We had a meeting with Geoff and outlined the project. He was enthusiastic and offered to assist in recruiting others to the scheme. It turned out that he had acquired a little brass cornet just like the one Buddy Bolden had, and welcomed the opportunity to press it into action. With his help we drew up a list of potential performers.

For the clarinet chair Paul Furniss was the obvious choice. An extremely able musician, Paul too has a deep understanding of New Orleans Jazz and its history. He also has the ability to perform with equal skill on Boehm and Albert (simple) system clarinets. Paul had some initial reservations about what was proposed, but agreed to listen to what we had to say.

Geoff suggested we talk to his friend banjo player Paul Finnerty who also plays Spanish Guitar. Geoff approached him on our behalf and he agreed hear what we had to say. He also suggested a number of possible bass violin players. We had to find someone who was not simply a slap bass player, someone who could really play the instrument with the bow. Eventually I telephoned Stan Valacos, one of the city's leading young jazz string players, who said he would meet with us.

We needed to find a trombonist who could play valve trombone and be able understand the role it played in the early bands. Trevor suggested John Bates, another very experienced jazz player. John also played tuba so we thought that background would stand him in good stead. As it turned out John had a valve trombone and was keen to hear about the project.

Trevor approached percussionist Ian Bloxsome. Ian plays jazz but also performs regularly in the opera orchestra at the Sydney Opera House. He is also something of a musicologist. He also had a calfskin head bass drum he thought would be appropriate.

Finding a violinist was not so easy. It was important to get a good reader with an understanding of jazz music. After much discussion it was agreed Trevor would talk to 18 year old Retaw Boyce who could play both swing style jazz and country fiddle. He was keen to hear more.

Because I thought we might be able to experiment with alternate formats including piccolo lead Trevor also spoke to the trombonist with his band Jim Elliott, a multi instrumentalist who plays the piccolo. Jim agreed come along to hear what I had to say.

Launching the Project

This initial reaction was very encouraging, but I realised that there was still a great deal that needed to be done to get the show on the road.

I arranged to have a meeting to clarify the historical background and establish the objectives and performance criteria for the project. I explained that what I had in mind was to establish a repertory orchestra that would be able to present concerts and make recordings replicating the jazz the period 1896/1907 with:

> Authentic instrumentation
> Contemporary repertoire
> Early Jazz performance practices

It looked like we would have instruments that, if they were not made in the 1890's, were at least of similar design, and the repertoire could be based straightforwardly on Bolden's known repertoire.

In trying to establish a style of performance we would have to apply the elements described in the previous chapter—melody-centred head arrangements, with individual variations on the theme. This meant understanding the traditional role of the violin and its effect on the balance of the front line instruments. This was something of a challenge for players whose experience was based on models from the 1920's or later. I later found a very succinct exposition of this problem by Lawrence

Gushee. Talking of reviving the music of the Original Creole Orchestra he wrote:

> "More than one musician has had the idea of "reviving" the Creole Band. Choosing a play list from the tunes mentioned above is only a faltering first step. A far more important step is to rid oneself of preconceived notions as to how a New Orleans ragtime band should play, how the various instruments should relate to one another on the basis of the Hot Five, say or the New Orleans revival bands of the 1940's. But most difficult of all is to devise an appropriate rhythmic style that's more than an unthinking adoption of the alternatives known from recordings of the 1920s and after."[141]

We would have to do all that. Fortunately there were ample clues available from the research that would help.

Rather than to try and replicate the sound of any one of the bands of the first generation I suggested we should try to play in a style that might have been played by a band with a mix of players of the time. We would not slavishly copy style models like Fred Keppard or Alphonse Picou but apply the lessons learned from their recorded performances to the music. Where we could identify habits of style that had been adopted from models that only appeared after 1917 we would eliminate them.

In respect of the rhythm we would apply what was known of "two-beat" style to those compositions in duple time. Three beat rhythm was to present its own series of problems as we explored the repertoire.

At the end of the first meeting it was agreed to set up a first rehearsal and John Bates volunteered to make a rehearsal space available in his home. Finding a suitable rehearsal time was from the beginning a problem. These were busy professional musicians making their services available in spare time. Nevertheless we made a start.

Rehearsals

From the first rehearsal we were faced with the need to grapple with problems that must have been encountered by the first faking bands.

---

141 Gushee L "Pioneers of Jazz" p291

I decided to make a start with some of the simpler tunes played by the Bolden Band. We began with *Funky Butt*.

Our violinist had to be able to play the melody role and that meant having a lead sheet. Jelly Roll Morton made several recordings of the tune as *Buddy Bolden's Blues* and his version has been published in written form. However witnesses suggested that Bolden played at a faster tempo, and Morton's versions are inflected with many of his own characteristic improvisations.

Another version appears as *King Bolden's Song* on a recording of the Louis James String Band[142] and this slightly more primitive melody line appeared more likely to be suitable as the basis of a lead sheet. That melody line was also a little closer to a theme of the contemporary piano rag *St. Louis Tickle* (a tune readers will recall Jelly Roll Morton thought was stolen from *Funky Butt*.) I also found a 1910 cylinder recording of the rag by the virtuoso banjo soloist Vess Ossman[143] that gave another slant on the melody, pace and rhythm of contemporary performance.

We decided it should be performed at a medium fast tempo.

In addition to the lead sheet I suggested a head arrangement that merely spelled out the order in which the lead would be taken by various instruments and included a chorus in which the horns play at low volume allowing the rhythmic impulse to come through.

Bolden's band apparently sang the words but the Eagle Band did not. However we decided to include vocal choruses, one of which would as far as possible reflect the original words. I found we had singers in the Orchestra who were prepared to give it a go.

Surprisingly, from the start, the players had little difficulty in adapting to the new style, but I found I had to listen differently to the blending of cornet and violin. It was a new sound.

However my simple notions of how the early musicians adapted to new material needed some revision. It was necessary to transpose piano scores to suit the Bb instruments and I was to find that the simple distinction between Fakers and Readers needed some adjustment. Some reading players wanted the melody written in treble clef, others in bass, some in concert pitch, others as for Bb pitch. Some relied entirely on chords, others wanted both lead sheet and chords. Some were ear players, who could read chords but wanted to hear the melody.

---

142 American Music CD AMCD-14
143 Lakeside Indestructible Cylinder Record no 318 also Yazoo LP L1044

There is, as far as I am aware, little or no information about how these things were managed in Bolden's time. There are a few clues. For example, Bunk Johnson said Bolden could play in any key but did not know in which key he was playing. Others said he would listen to a tune, memorize it, and then teach it to others.

However once these problems were worked out we began to make some progress in playing through the repertoire.

Other commitments led to Trevor Rippingale and Jim Elliott being unable to continue to participate after a short time and our young violinist also had to leave for reasons unconnected with the project.

Fortunately, bass player Stan Valacos recommended Daniel Weltlinger a skilled jazz violinist and Dan agreed to take over the role.

Concert Performances

By the first quarter of 2005 the group was playing with some confidence and I was delighted when an old friend, the blues singer Kate Dunbar, a member of the Sydney Jazz Club board phoned and asked if we could perform for the club later in the year. It was agreed that to celebrate Buddy Bolden's Birthday we would play for the club's September monthly meeting. Buddy was born on 6th September but the club meets on Friday nights so we agreed on Friday 9th September 2005.

Coincidentally John Buchanan, another old friend from my days playing at the Sydney Jazz Club, who promotes Jazz Concerts, asked if we could take part in a New Orleans Revival concert featuring Geoff Bull's Olympia Jazz Band also to be held in September. It was agreed we would play the first set of the Legends of Jazz concert to be held on 22nd September.

We were hardly ready to perform a whole concert program and it was made more difficult because Dan Weltlinger had committed to a three-month tour in Europe and Geoff Bull too was to go to play at the Ascona jazz festival and other venues on the continent. In addition, Ian Bloxsome found that as he was likely to be committed to Opera performances he could not guarantee to make the September date, and recommended an up and coming young drummer, Anthony Howe, to replace him. This worked out well.

We could not rehearse until Geoff returned in late July but Retaw Boyce found he could return, and kindly agreed to stand in on violin as soon as Geoff returned. This gave the other members some much needed rehearsal time before Dan returned in early August. With his arrival, an intensive schedule of rehearsals was undertaken. We were nearly ready.

Fig.16 Above: The Buddy Bolden Revival Orchestra at the Sydney Jazz Club 9th September 2005
Left to right: Dan Hardie, Paul Finnerty, Stan Valacos, Paul Furniss (face obscured), Dan Weltlinger, Anthony Howe (obscured), Geoff Bull, John Bates.

Our concert for the Sydney Jazz Club on 9th September 2005 was somewhat dampened by the impact on New Orleans of hurricane Katrina, which many in the audience and the orchestra felt deeply. Nevertheless it went well.

The performance was accompanied by a computer slide presentation. Because many jazz supporters are not very knowledgeable about Buddy Bolden and his times I gave a brief introduction to the Bolden story and introduced the band and its mission.

I also introduced each number, giving a short account of its history and significance. The following compositions were included:

Don't Go Way Nobody
Funky Butt
Moonwinks Mazurka

Any Rags
If You Don't Shake
La Praline Quadrille
Makin' Runs
Make Me a Pallet on the Floor
Ride On King Jesus
Careless Love Blues
My Bucket's Got a Hole in It
The Maple Leaf Rag
Home Sweet Home

A slightly shorter programme was presented at John Buchanan's New Orleans Revival Concert on 22nd September but this time I was able to have a tape recording made of the performance. (See footnote below.) [144]

Unfortunately we were forced to abandon a concert performance planned for April 2006 because of pressing overseas commitments, and a series of recording sessions planned for the early part of the year was also aborted because other commitments prevented us getting all the players together at the same time. It is hoped that should further concert opportunities appear we would be able to extend the performance repertoire beyond the 20 compositions we have played through to date.

---

[144] Note: Clips from the tape may be heard via the internet at the Buddy Bolden Revival Orchestra's web page that can be accessed from the Author's Home Page at: **http://members.ozemail.com.au/~darnhard/EarlyJazzHistory.html**

Chapter 8

Not Quite Ragtime

"The band was probably much lighter in sound than many descriptions of it would indicate. They must have played with more strength than the downtown bands, but the rhythm section, bowed bass and guitar, was light, and the band probably had an almost Spanish flavor"

—Sam Charters

A member of the audience at one of our concerts spoke to me after the performance. He said: "You know its not quite jazz and not quite ragtime." Another asked: "Isn't it a bit like parlour music?" All I could say was: "It's the nearest we can get to the first syncopated jazz style—somewhere on the border between 19th Century popular music and 1917 Dixieland jazz."

What made our performances different from recreations of instrumental ragtime made by groups like the New Orleans Ragtime Orchestra is that they were improvised at all times. How authentic they were depended on the extent we were able to conform to the principles of performance practice outlined in a previous chapter.

The Melody Based Ensemble Style

In general the melody was kept going by the violin and the lead was passed around among the horn players accompanied by the whole band playing variations on the melody, harmony or ad lib riffs. There were a few occasions when this was forgotten, and one or more players dropped out, but these were exceptions.

The cornet ragged the tune in ensemble passages throwing in runs, doubling notes, shortening and lengthening them ad lib. Individual breaks were inserted at convenient places in the melody. In ensemble passages the clarinet played what John St Cyr described as 'obbligato, second or side melody'—or harmony.

When the lead was passed to clarinet or trombone they dutifully limited their variations to elaboration or embellishment of the melody. Audiences used to present day jazz performers may have found this perplexing but they still applauded the 'soloist'.

John Bates on valve trombone took quickly to the two-beat vamp based style, and previous brass band experience clearly assisted him in adapting to the role of providing bass support; but sometimes "filled in open spots, played harmony with another horn and sometimes took the lead."[145] One audience member said that the rhythmic impulse he provided was what drove the rhythm section.

How it Sounds

In testing our head arrangements we quickly became aware of the different sound values created by the addition of instruments not normally included in a present day jazz band. The sound is determined partly by the instruments used; partly by the way they are played, and partly by the composition being performed.

I admit I initially found it hard to imagine what the sound might be like and how it might differ from that of a modern traditional jazz band. I believe others had the same problem. John Bates said he thought the concert recordings sounded authentic. How do you judge authenticity when there is no original recording for comparison? Let's begin with description.

Instrumental Voicing

The balance of sound between the louder frontline/instruments and the violin was, as expected, an issue.

Writing in the 1960's Johnny St.Cyr said:

---

[145] Bebe Ridgeley see Chapter 3

"... brass instruments did not play as loud as they do in these days."

Our brass players did not play particularly loudly, but even so, in many passages the individual violin line was difficult to observe. However, when playing melody in the upper register, the violin added a fourth front-line voice above the cornet that added a spicy upper edge to the overall sound. This can also be perceived in some of the recordings of Piron's New Orleans Orchestra made in 1923. Sometimes it was difficult to distinguish whether upper register phrases were being played by clarinet or violin. This is also apparent in the Piron Orchestra recordings.

The addition of the violin, often playing above the stave, changed the overall pitch and sonority of the ensemble. In ensemble passages this creates shriller more high-pitched sound. When the violin takes the lead, with other instruments ragging or harmonising, the sound often has a pronounced (19th Century) parlour music quality. Also, with the cornet (which sounds sweeter than the 20th century trumpet) blending with the violin the overall sound is sweeter than the trumpet based sound of today, reminding us of Baby Dodds' observation when describing the role of the violin in performance that:

'The way we used to play a long time ago sounded awful sweet.'[146]

The inclusion of the violin playing ragged melodies, as written, in ragtime era sheet music sometimes also added an extra contrapuntal voice in the front line creating a swing or rock we had not anticipated. This was particularly noticeable in the raggy choruses of Coon Song era compositions like *Any Rags*.

Additionally we discovered that, in the blues, the violin played in the context of the early jazz style has a plangent individual voice.

Comparison with the Piron Orchestra recordings, particularly the recording of *West Indies Blues* made with singer Esther Bigeou, suggests we were close to the early four-piece front line sound. I have suggested elsewhere that these recordings may represent a survival of the early jazz sound, despite the addition of saxophones in many arrangements.[147] We did not, however, set out to emulate the Piron group.

---

146 in Russel W. "New Orleans Style"
147 Piron's New Orleans Orchestra CD Azure AZCD 13

Sound Balance

Problems of sound balance were complicated by the size of present day concert venues, and the ever-present permanent sound set-ups, where a professional soundman sets out microphones and makes his own sound balance arrangements. Amplifying the brass instruments and clarinet further disadvantaged the violin and other stringed rhythm instruments until amplification of those instruments was boosted. In these circumstances it can hardly be regarded as an authentic recreation of the original New Orleans sound as played in the smaller venues like the *Funky Butt Hall*. This problem is also encountered in the recording studio and we are yet to find a satisfactory resolution. It is easy enough to balance the sound to bring forward violin, bass and guitar, but this does not necessarily create an authentic sound. Our current challenge is to make recordings of the group that adequately reflect the original character of Elemental Jazz. Even with a one microphone set-up instrumental placement to achieve an authentic balance may prove difficult to achieve.

Similarly the bass violin played with the bow was a new experience, particularly as the earliest jazz recordings did not include the string bass. Mark Katz suggested that this was due to limitations in the early recording methods:

> "the double bass ... played at the edge of recordability ... the problem was that the high frequencies created by the attack of the bow were suppressed. Without a clear attack the sound is muddified and not even clearly identified as coming from a bass"

He went on to suggest that this limitation led to the adoption of the slap bass technique:

> "which gives the bass a more percussive and concentrated sound."[148]

We experienced this problem too, unless the bass is played at the bottom of its range. It can be overcome using modern multi microphone recording techniques and providing bass amplification, but this is hardly an accurate reproduction of the original sound. The effect can be heard on Humphrey Lyttleton's Calligraph Bolden Era recordings of

---

148 Katz M. "Capturing Sound—How Technology has Changed Music" 2004 p 82

the late 1980's. It is explained in his video account of this experiment. It is a problem yet to be solved.

Rhythm and Instrumentation

Other instrumental effects soon became apparent. For example, the bass violin played with the bow creates a new low throbbing bass line, but does not propel the rhythm to the same extent as the 'oompah' of the later slap bass. In practice, in the absence of the piano, the guitar tends to come forward as a major propulsive after beat component of the rhythm section. This is clearly heard in quiet passages of recordings, and very apparent to the other instrumentalists. Baby Dodds commented that in his view the inclusion of the guitar, (without a piano) in the rhythm section made for a sweeter sounding jazz band.[149] This appears to be correct. Sam Charters suggestion that the rhythm section with bowed bass and guitar was light appears also to be justified.

The valve trombone played a bass support role in early bands and our experience suggests that, in ensemble passages, the rather light rhythm section (without banjo or piano) is enhanced by the support of vigorous ragtime-like trombone vamps, (rather like what has been called the "Boom Chick Bass" usually written for the ragtime pianist's left hand in turn of the century sheet music[150]). Roy Palmer who played trombone with the Rozelle Orchestra in 1905 said that in the old time style the trombonist should vamp whenever possible, stressing the after beats and always getting back to vamping after excursions into melody or harmony.[151]

This type of vamping bass was also written in to the trombone parts of many ragtime orchestral arrangements including some by Scott Joplin and the piano scores of many popular ragtime songs of the time.

The flexibility of the valve trombone also facilitated the tracing of the more complex ragtime era melody lines when the theme was passed to the trombonist. On the other hand the valve trombone proved less able to produce rough breaks and blues inflections than its slide counterpart.

According to Brian Wood:

---

149 Dodds and Gara op cit p13
150 See Berlin E.A. "Ragtime a Musical and Cultural History" 1980
151 Russel W. op cit p133

"Lorenzo Tio explained the concept of "split time" to Barney Bigard, in which New Orleans front line musicians would tie their phrasing to two beats to the bar, hence the tag of "two-beat" used for Dixieland jazz, in which string bass or tuba players would accent beats one and three in a measure. However, as early as 1907 Bill Johnson was coupling the two beat feel to a four in a bar propulsion which added a rhythmic exchange in the backwards and forwards flow between front line and rhythm section. Baby Dodds' drumming provided a near perfect example of this characteristic: even when playing a march the four beat accents combine with the tune's natural two in a bar displacements. Alternatively, listen to Lu Watters with and without Bunk: the former plods; the latter swings."

We found this tying of the melody to rhythm to be the correct approach, and it explains to some extent the observation that it is not quite ragtime but not quite jazz.

Experimenting with Instrumental Formats

As indicated in an earlier chapter there was an initial period of time during which the early jazz bands experimented with format. We know that Buddy Bolden substituted a second clarinet for the violin at some stage. Witnesses suggested that this was a temporary expedient when violinist Alcide Frank left to form his own Golden Rule Orchestra. Alcide Frank's brother, piccolo and flute player Gilbert "Bab" Frank performed as leader of the Peerless Orchestra and later of the Eagle Band. He seems also to have played in the Tuxedo Orchestra around 1910—a group that also had a violin player.

I originally proposed experimenting with both two-clarinet and piccolo lead formats. As it turned out this was probably too ambitious. However we did make some initial efforts to do so.

The two-clarinet formula proved impossible to implement. Clarinet players who developed their style of performance in traditional jazz are not really as suited as violinists to adopting the melody lead role.

In the 1980's the English bandleader Humphrey Lyttleton made a series of recreational recordings using a second clarinet to carry the melody.[152] Though he briefly instructed the player using C clarinet in the melody role, the result featured competing upper register clarinet runs and cross currents rather more than a melody centred style. (Jelly Roll Morton said that in Fred Keppard's band the clarinet played the melody in a lower register.) I believe the experiment might be more successful with a lead clarinet player with a classical or brass band background and little jazz exposure.

Lyttleton's use of the C clarinet was probably authentic but the pitch of the instrument also led to a shriller overall sound than that created with the softer voice of the violin. I intended to try the C clarinet as lead but unfortunately my C clarinet proved to be a high pitch instrument that could not be brought in tune with the Bb instruments.

We did have some success with the piccolo, though we were unable to continue to use it over an extended period. In particular we substituted the piccolo for the violin in a rehearsal performance of *Makin' Runs*—the march-like tune attributed to Bolden by Bunk Johnson. Though the piccolo was even shriller than the C clarinet it concentrated on the melodic theme and it contributed a spritely rhythmic impulse. I would have liked to carry these experiments further but we concluded it was more important to get the most from the violin-led set up.

Vocal Choruses

The Bolden orchestra appears to have featured extempore vocal contributions by members of the band though there is little information about whether they sang ensembles or as individuals. We decided to include vocal choruses in head arrangements of tunes like *Funky Butt* and *Any Rags*. However we did not to attempt to imitate the regional New Orleans Afro-American accent though an accurate recreation should preferably do so; nor did we imitate the pseudo slave patois inherent in early Coon Song lyrics. To this extent these performances fall short of ideal reconstructions and they would be improved if a New Orleans Afro-American vocalist could be persuaded to participate.

While it is clear that Bolden's audiences were prepared to accept songs like *If the Man In the Moon Were a Coon* it is uncertain whether they would have interpreted the lyrics of these parody songs as writ-

---

152 Calligraph LP CLGLP 01 and BBC TV video recording "Buddy Bolden's Children"

ten, or simply re-interpreted them in their normal local dialect. I believe they might have done the latter.

It is interesting to hear the vocal performance of *Any Rags* by Johnny St. Cyr recorded by Wooden Joe Nicholas Band in 1945. In this he sings his very loose interpretation of the lyric of the chorus in a fairly uninflected way. We chose to follow his lead.

There is a story that in the 1940's, when bandleader Tommy Dorsey recorded *If the Man In the Moon Were a Coon* his vocalist was very reluctant to sing the song and only did so under threat of dismissal from his leader.

The Vernacular Style

Listening to performances of that part of the repertoire that had origins in street and folk music the sound is different; much closer to that of more recent jazz bands, less 'ragtimey'.

This was probably to be expected. As time progressed the Coon Songs and Cakewalks dropped out of the repertoire though many of the blues oriented compositions have remained until the present day. We tried to incorporate in these performances the style elements witnesses attributed to the Bolden band. The result was a blend of folk blues and spiritual elements that was particularly noticeable in the converted spirituals like *Ride on King (Jesus)*, which had call and response figures built into verse and chorus and provided opportunities to insert breaks. The result was a jubilee-like transformation; a snappy, bouncy, stomp, without the Coon Song flavour, but not quite a blues. In these pieces hot syncopated cross rhythms sometimes appeared quite naturally.

Triple Time

Very few jazz bands have made recordings that were not in duple[153] (2/4) or quadruple[154] (4/4) time. Most ragtime compositions were written in duple time. This should not be confused with two-beat rhythm, in which (in quadruple time), stresses are placed on the first and third

---

153 Two beats to the measure
154 Four beats to the measure

beats by bass drum and string bass, but accentuated on second and third beats by the snare drum and guitar. In four-beat rhythm all four beats are stressed evenly (Unfortunately the local practice among New Orleans jazz musicians has been to refer to two-beat rhythm as 'two-four' and four-beat as 'four-four'.)

Bands in the Bolden era usually played two-beat rhythm in tunes in quadruple time. This included marches and many songs. A good example of two-beat drumming can be heard in the recording of *Come On and Stomp Stomp Stomp* by Johnny Dodds Black Bottom Stompers.[155]

Some New Orleans performers, notably George Lewis recorded waltzes in triple time (3/4) but usually only as a prelude to swinging them into a hot four-beat jazzed up performance. Nevertheless such performances do give some idea of how the waltz might have been performed by early jazz musicians.

The Buddy Bolden Revival Orchestra had no difficulty adapting to the two-beat rhythm but many of the dances performed in the Bolden Era were danced in three beat time (3/4) or a compound time called 6/8.

Waltzes and Mazurkas usually required 3/4 times, Schottisches 4/4 and, in the early days, Two-steps were danced in 6/8. However by 1900 many Two-steps were being danced in 4/4 ragtime March tempo.

Waltzes, Mazurkas, and Schottisches Polkas were new to us. Research into musical history provided some clues as to performance practice. Historically, for example, waltzes relied on an emphasis on the first beat of the bar, and similar information was available about Mazurkas, Schottisches and Polkas. Information was also available about the speed of performance. (Johnny St. Cyr said the tempo of *Sentimental Journey* was ideal for the Schottische as danced in New Orleans).

Sometimes the score was of help. For example, the chorus of *Lazy Moon* contains a number of four-note 'dotted' sequences, often called Schottische figures, which give a clue to how it should be performed. A contemporary arrangement of the Three-Step Moonwinks *Mazurka* provided by the Tulane University Jazz Archive clearly indicated how the clarinet might have played in an improvised performance. I also found a 1909 cylinder recording of *Moonwinks* by banjoist Vess Ossman with orchestral accompaniment[156]. In the case of *La Praline* we had Jelly Roll

---

155 Classics CD 617 D
156 Edison Standard Record 10112

Morton's recorded demonstration of the various performance styles to assist.

With all that behind us I decided that we should in general try to prepare as Bolden might have done. That is to say, we should produce a lead sheet and apply the principles of melody centred improvisation we were already applying to the two-beat numbers. The result was a style of performance much closer to the parlour music mode, but still improvised. In some of these head arrangements the violin played a significant part, supporting the cornet and maintaining the melodic structure. There was also scope for the cornet and trombone to reinforce the third and fourth beats of the measure, leaving the violin and clarinet to 'variate' the tune or harmonise a theme.

A certain amount of swing or sway emerged as the performances developed and this was most noticeable in the Polka section of *La Praline*.

The music was also sweeter—more sentimental. Trombonist Bill Matthews said:

> "When it came to playing sweet music; waltzes, there was nobody in the country that could touch him ... He was one of the sweetest trumpet players on waltzes ... Everybody was crazy about Bolden when he'd blow a waltz, schottische or old low down blues.[157]

That is not now hard to believe.

We didn't know how jazz audiences would react to these early dance settings. The performers enjoyed the challenge and began to appreciate delicate compositions like *Moonwinks* for their own sake. As it turned out, concert audiences responded enthusiastically as they began to get a glimpse of social dancing in the New Orleans of 1900.

Hot Ragtime

The reason audiences associated our performances with ragtime is, I believe, the two-beat rhythm in close association with the syncopated melody lines common to the popular Coon Songs and cakewalks of the period 1895-1900. This combination, which predates ragtime, is prob-

---

[157] HJA March 1959

ably derived from earlier minstrel performances and even earlier slave secular songs and dances.

This is, perhaps, the reason Jelly Roll Morton said Bolden played ragtime and blues. His repertoire contained a considerable proportion of these popular songs and Morton perhaps considered them old-fashioned.

The more complex multi-thematic piano rags of Scott Joplin and his school that appeared after 1899 were a smaller proportion of his repertoire and a quite different kind of composition. They faced the new improvising bands with problems.

We decided apply the principles of melody centred performance to the Classic Rags in the repertoire. It was not simply a matter of reading the piano score, though the violinist could readily do so.

They were often written in keys that appeared difficult for the Bb instruments. (Some brass players do find some of the remoter flat keys easy to perform in, though this places additional demands on the clarinet.) Some themes were written high above the stave—too high for the cornet, so a certain amount of judicious re-assignment of solos and simplification of melody lines was needed. Some of the more intricate themes are also difficult for non-reading players to learn. In particular James Scott's *Frog Legs Rag* proved something of a challenge.

However we were able to adapt compositions like *Maple Leaf Rag* fairly easily to the improvising style.

On the whole I wonder about including such classic rags in the Bolden repertoire. There are a number of witnesses who said Bolden could not perform them and they might be right. His contemporary Manuel Perez certainly did. In the next ten years, however, they were to be increasingly adapted in a hot free ragtime manner, becoming one of the foundations of Dixieland and the music of the Jazz Age. (Samuel Charters called this free ragtime played by second-generation bands like those of Jack Carey and Kid Ory 'spontaneous orchestral ragtime'.)

Authenticity

Readers might reasonably assume from the above that I am reasonably happy with the authenticity of what we have done. There are some things I would yet like to do if time permits.

I would like, for example, to have restrung each of the stringed instruments with gut strings, as steel strings were not available in the early 1900's. However this was too costly, working as we were on a budget of $0.

As indicated above I would like to have recorded a greater proportion of the repertoire. We may yet do so.

Some other groups have chosen to play rougher, or hammed it up, presumably on the assumption that the music of Bolden's time was like that. There are suggestions that Bolden played rough at times, but there are strong indications that the music that was played was alternately loud and soft and sometimes very sweet. The few rough spots in our concert performances were also perhaps typical of early improvisation and therefore authentic.

Chapter 9

Historically Informed Performance

"One might say that for the jazz historian the recording is analogous to the musical manuscript (or letter or archival document) for the academic musicologist examining the European musical past."

—L. Gushee[158]

When archaeologists are excavating a site of early habitation they collect and catalogue all the artefacts found during the dig and draw up a plan of the site on which they locate the remnants of buildings and other structures. By that stage they have usually begun to formulate hypotheses about the dating, purposes and form of the settlement. At this stage it is common practice to develop an architectural sketch or model to illuminate or visualise details of location and reconstruct the structures; hopefully bringing their history to life. These days elaborate computer simulations are used to synthesise their findings creating a virtual reconstruction.

In previous works, I have sought to apply an approach described in the introduction to Alex Wilder's history of American Popular Music as "contemplative study that would go beyond research to imaginative reconstruction based upon archaeological analogy."[159]

Much of the research data about early jazz history has already been published, scattered in various publications; histories; biographies and autobiographies and some remains in accessible form in the jazz archives of New Orleans Tulane Universities. What was needed was to

---

158 Gushee L. op cit p15
159 Wilder A. "American Popular Music" Introduction

assemble this information in an accurate historical and temporal matrix that located the major developments and contributors in time. This work was largely completed and published in *Exploring Early Jazz—The Origins and Evolution of the New Orleans Style*.

There were some obvious gaps in the published data, the most glaring being the absence of a coherent account of white jazz in New Orleans before about 1910. Another lacuna—the missing history of the Original Creole Orchestra has now been eliminated following the publication of Lawrence Gushee's 2005 publication *Pioneers of Jazz-The Story of the Creole Band*.

Recordings and Early Jazz History

I have previously promoted the notion that the absence of recorded examples of jazz before 1917 need not impede the development of an accurate history of its earliest stage.

Gushee considered the traditional emphasis on discography among jazz historians a considerable limitation:

> "This fundamental bias must be one of the roots of neglect of the Creole Band in the history of jazz, even now that more and more works of scholarship using as wide as possible range of sources have been written. Even so, considering the amount of speculative prose devoted to Charles "Buddy" Bolden—the alleged father of jazz, who also left no recordings, even from his later career—the neglect is strange."[160]

If Charles Edward Smith had found the fabled cylinder recording of the Bolden Orchestra the story of the group would no doubt have had a greater legitimacy among earlier historical writers. Nevertheless recordings have been the major means of transmission of the jazz tradition.

In their absence many writers have presumed that we can never know how the early music sounded, and such was the power of the phonograph that whole generations could be forgiven for believing that jazz came into existence in 1917 with the first recordings.

Gushee pointedly remarked:

---

160 Gushee L. op cit p15

"One might say that Jazz writers have no need to consider issues such as the ones mentioned above. They can rely on "ostensive definition", as though the answer to the question "what is jazz?" is to point to a record (or better yet, play it).

However, in the absence of the magical recording, it was studious and painstaking traditional historical research by Donald M. Marquis[161] that lifted the clouds of myth surrounding Bolden and clarified his contribution to the beginnings of jazz.

Having established from their research a model of the musical style of, say the time of J.S. Bach, the founders early music movement proceeded to apply the performance practices they identified to concert performances, and subsequently, to widely disseminated recordings. Consequently there has been a revolution in the understanding and appreciation of his music, and of early music generally.

Similarly, once we had established from the research the critical elements that defined early jazz performance as outlined in Chapter 6, our rehearsal programme provided a similar opportunity to test them and prepare for concert performances in the old style; our archaeologist's model of early jazz, if you like.

What We Learned

Some years ago I had a brief discussion with New Orleans researcher Dr. Jack Stewart about Bolden's music. He suggested it was important to study the published music of Bolden's time. Similarly when I asked Donald Marquis for his ideas on the matter he suggested I look at the sheet music being advertised in the local press of the day. As it turned out, both were valuable suggestions. Jelly Roll Morton said he found tunes to play from those advertised in the Sunday Papers.

In the course of preparing for our rehearsal schedule considerable insight was gained into the music of the time.

As indicated in earlier chapters it was discovered that unlike the recorded 4/4 jazz music of the 1920's there was a considerable variety of rhythmic material. It was a music of transition, somewhere between the popular songs and parlour music of the 19th century and the blues

---

161 Marquis D. op cit 19781993

oriented uptown street songs. Accordingly the repertoire split into two seemingly quite different sections.

However by applying the reported performance practices of the time to each of the compositions we found a consistent style that merged the differences. We found the same robust method could be effective in bringing to life Coon Song, Waltz, Mazurka and Quadrille.

We also learned that the instrumentation was practicable. Far from being a disruptive influence, the violin provided continuity, allowing the cornet to rag freely around the melody. We rediscovered the voice of the violin, a sound largely lost during the recorded era. The light rhythm section was effective, and the trombone, playing vamps, supplemented the rhythmic impulse. The sound was hot "sweet soft plenty rhythm".[162]

What is in a Name?

The exercise of preparing and playing through the better part of the repertoire also brought into focus some of the weak spots in the evidence of early musicians. Notably that of Jelly Roll Morton who while being very specific at times made some statements apparently in conflict with other evidence. Morton described Bolden's Band as playing ragtime and blues but not jazz. He claimed he invented jazz in 1902 and promoted Freddie Keppard as the first true jazz cornet player (1907/8). This conflicts with evidence from other witnesses, like Peter Bocage, who said Bolden played jazz. Others claimed the younger Keppard played like Bolden. It seems that this, like many similar discontinuities in the evidence about early jazz is largely a dispute about the meanings of words.

I note that in a recent article Jack Stewart quoted a number of witnesses who told him the first band to play jazz was the Original Dixieland Jazz Band. He quoted bandleader Johnny Dedroit who told him that Buddy Bolden and "all the other people all played ragtime":

> "I asked him what he meant by ragtime and he said all the popular pieces the bands played ... I asked him what the local interpretation of ragtime sounded like and he

---

[162] Jelly Roll Morton in Lomax A. "Mr Jelly Roll" 1952 p 64

said that, 'It was a nice lilting music if you like that sort of thing, but it wasn't jazz.'"[163]

Dedroit clearly saw jazz as something new in 1917, not an unreasonable view, because this was the first time the word was used to describe the music.

Richard Collins also saw the white jazz of 1917 as a departure from the earlier New Orleans Style that he associated with the skilled Creole musicians of the day. He described jazz as:

"... a formularised sound produced by white routineer bands that have no understanding of music."[164]

He wrote:

"... routineers fashioned a routine usually consisting of a verse, chorus and one or two variation choruses."[165]

In an oral history interview Nick La Rocca was asked what New Orleans bands were playing before 1917:

"Well they all played ragtime ... the bands they all played regular popular tunes. And I never heard any numbers that was improvised or worked on. If they played a chorus, they may have add a lil'bit flourishes to 'em of their own. I don't say they didn't do that; but they were playing ragtime."[166]

He went on to claim that jazz arrived in Chicago because the new Fox-trot could not be danced to the customary New Orleans beat. Unfortunately he was completely confused about what the beat was and how it was changed. To quote Jack Stewart:

"La Rocca says they changed from four beats to two beats, whereas the reverse is what actually happened."[167]

---

163 Stewart J. "The Original Dixieland Jazz Band's Place in the History of Jazz" the Jazz Archivist vol xix 2005/6 p17
164 Collins op cit p237
165 Collins op cit p236
166 Stewart J. "The Original Dixieland Jazz Band's place in the History of Jazz" the Jazz Archivist vol xix 2005/6 p21
167 Stewart J. "The Original Dixieland Jazz Band's place in the History of Jazz" the Jazz Archivist vol xix 2005/6 p22

Stewart demonstrates quite clearly that the music was changed from two-beat to four-four because the Fox-trot could not be danced comfortably to the old New Orleans two-beat rhythm. He quoted Virgil Thomson writing in 1924:

> "Jazz, in brief is (a) a compound of the fox-trot rhythm, a four-four measure (*alla breve*) with a double accent, and (b) a syncopated melody over the rhythm. Neither alone will make jazz. The monotonous fox-trot rhythm, by itself will either put you to sleep or drive you mad."

I noticed that at our Sydney Jazz Club concert, where dancing was a regular feature of Club meetings, the dancers were uncomfortable when trying to dance to the two-beat rhythm and quite nonplussed by the Mazurka.

Morton (in 1902) and La Rocca (in 1917) both claimed the title inventor of jazz but they appear to agree that those New Orleans bands that played improvised popular tunes were playing ragtime, though Morton said that Bolden played ragtime and blues. Morton seemed to see the absence of Spanish rhythm as a limitation of ragtime and a necessary feature of jazz. He claimed the right to define jazz, and did so retrospectively in the early Swing Era, when his own style was becoming old-fashioned and some unkind writers described him as a ragtime player. Unfortunately Morton's 'definition' of jazz is scattered among written and recorded accounts of his conversations with Alan Lomax and others. Nevertheless, almost all of the features he described as essential can be found in accounts of the Elemental Jazz Style. Both Morton and La Rocca thought they were playing jazz.

It is clear that any definition of jazz is time sensitive. Thomson's definition undoubtedly described the jazz of 1924, but could not have done so at a later time. Similarly, numerous witnesses ascribe the beginnings of jazz to around 1900, though the word could not then have been applied to it.

Our exploration of the tunes played by the Bolden band showed that those that were called ragtime were, in fact, syncopated popular songs that were known as ragtime after 1900. Some were still Coon Songs, others sentimental ballads, both forms derived from an earlier stream of theatrical and musical development.[168]

---

[168] The relationship between ragging, syncopation and the evolution of the popular song is well described Morgan and Barlow op cit p 21

Classical ragtime was another matter. After 1899 composers published multi-thematic pieces called rags. They were all similar in form and many readers of today associate the term Ragtime with this sort of composition. As we have seen this type of work did not comprise a considerable proportion of the Bolden repertoire and some witnesses said he did not play them. There is evidence, however, that some of the first generation bands played written arrangements of Classical Rags, notably the Imperial Orchestra associated with Manuel Perez, and there were other New Orleans dance bands that played only written arrangements including presumably those of Classic rags. One of the first of the early 'tin bands' (the Silver Leaf Orchestra) continued this tradition. This literal performance of written ragtime era music cannot reasonably be called jazz. While recognising the later influence of ragtime on early jazz, I have been reluctant to use the term ragtime to describe it as I think it has been a most misleading usage.

The Spanish Tinge

Numerous commentators mention the possible influence of so called Spanish Rhythms and this cannot be dismissed. Most commonly they refer to the syncopated tangana[169] or habanera rhythm.

Jelly Roll Morton said that it was an essential element of jazz melody, notably absent from hot ragtime, and demonstrated how it needed to be incorporated as syncopation in the pianist's right hand, using his *New Orleans Blues* written in 1902 as an example.

In a paper published on the Potomac River Jazz Club Internet site Don Rouse explored such rhythmic influences in numerous New Orleans jazz recordings. He particularly stressed that both Caribbean music and New Orleans jazz contain what he called a 'multiple overlay of cross-rhythms'—rhythmic accents falling ahead or behind the regular meter.[170]

Rouse indicated that guitarist Danny Barker said he learned this style of playing from Lorenzo Staultz who played with Bolden's Band and in Frank Duson's Eagle Band. Barker wrote about Bolden in a number of publications and often stated that the Bolden band would play Spanish

---

169 Tangana was the word used by W.C. Handy to describe the habanera rhythm.
170 New Orleans Jazz and Caribbean Music 2002 (www.prjc.org)

rhythms in soft passages when playing the blues. John Storm Roberts noted that Barker's description:

> "... suggests the passages for percussion called *rumbones* that are still part of salsa today."[171]

Listening to the *Buddy Bolden Revival Orchestra* in rehearsal I noted many occasions when this seemed to be occurring naturally and it became very noticeable when playing the chorus of *Under the Bamboo Tree*. This is because habanera like rhythms are actually written into the melody line of the chorus and superimposed on an habanesque bass rhythm identical with that of the published piano score of Morton's tango flavoured *New Orleans Blues*.

Some time ago I came across a cylinder recording made in 1906 in Cuba by the Orquesta Pablo Valenzuela[172] entitled *La Patti Negra*[173] the chorus of which is substantially the same as that of *Under the Bamboo Tree*. This early performance bears a remarkable similarity to later New Orleans jazz and it may be the earliest Cuban recording to demonstrate common features with the early New Orleans style, including the violin lead. In 1906 Bolden was still playing.

In a recent article John Doheny has demonstrated how the "swing feel" caused by differently accented eighth notes in New Orleans jazz create a rhythm identical to that of the Afro Cuban *tresillo*.[174]

John Storm Roberts commented that:

> "Despite Morton's theories, the Spanish tinge was by no means missing from ragtime ... the habanera's ritmo de tango was virtually identical with the cakewalk rhythm—and in fact, both are versions of a rhythmic motif common in a wide range of Afro-American music."[175]

---

171 13 Roberts J.S. "The Latin Tinge" 1979/99 p38
172 The Cuban Danzon—Arhoolie 7032
173 Named after the soprano Sissieretta Jones the "Black Patti" who worked with Cole and Johnson writers of *Under the Bamboo Tree*.
174 Doheny J. "The Spanish Tinge Hypothesis" in The Jazz Archivist Vol xix 2005/6 p14ff
175 Roberts J.S. "The Latin Tinge" 1979/99 p39

Variations in Performance Practice

Not all the bands of the first jazz generation played exactly the same way. Johnny St Cyr said he thought Alcide Frank's Golden Rule Band was hotter than the Bolden Band. Unfortunately we have little other information about it. Perez' Imperial Orchestra adhered to the written arrangements but usually had some players who improvised. Perez was not a strong improviser and had to have his breaks written out for him. Perez' band used a slide trombone presumably reading the score.

This seems to suggest some variety in their approaches to preparing a number. I conducted an experiment to test the feasibility of combining improvised and literal performance. I asked Paul Furniss to play the written part from a contemporary arrangement of *Moonwinks* while the rest of the group performed our usual improvised head arrangement.

It proved quite informative, particularly as I later discovered that the same clarinet part seems to have been used in Vess Ossman's 1909 cylinder recording of that mazurka. Paul told me he thought the part was similar to what he would normally have played when improvising and it was not detectable that he was not doing so.

Similarly our short lived experiment with the piccolo lead shed light on another of the variety of options available to the early jazz bands. There are suggestions that Bab Frank played piccolo lead in the hot Golden Rule Band before 1900 and certainly he was leading the more conventional Peerless Orchestra by 1906. An early photo of that group shows him with both piccolo and flute, presumably leading from the violin part. Not long after that he was leading Frank Duson's Eagle Band. He seems to have played in the Tuxedo Orchestra around 1910, a group that also had a violinist and he also played with John Robichaux's violin led orchestra. As late as the 1920's he was playing with a New Orleans band led by clarinettist Laurence Duhé (Dewey) in Chicago.

Although Bolden's experiment with two clarinets does not appear to have been copied by other first generation bands there are reports of later groups using two clarinets. Laurence Duhé mentioned an engagement at which he played what he called the reading part while Sydney Bechet (a non-reader) played the hot part. Fortunately Humphrey Lyttleton's 1980's recreation experiment sought to replicate this format, although as mentioned in an earlier chapter, I would like to repeat the exercise with a modified role for the melody clarinet.

We introduced the slide trombone in the last section of the Quadrille *La Praline* to illustrate the transition to the tailgate slide trombone style that occurred around 1912/13 in the bands of Jack Carey and Kid Ory. Carey is reputed to have converted the last movement of the Quadrille to a syncopated feature for slide trombone known as *Play Jack Carey* and called by white bands *Nigger No 2*. A truncated version of the Quadrille was later copyrighted by the Original Dixieland Jazz Band as *Tiger Rag*. As we have seen, Jelly Roll Morton also claimed he converted the last section of the Quadrille to *Tiger Rag*. As one might expect, the introduction of the slide trombone energised the performance much to the delight of audiences.

Interestingly, the first recording made by a black New Orleans band was actually an adaptation a ragtime era tune *(Carbarlick Acid)* that featured an added introduction that included showy tailgate slide trombone breaks. That was the Kid Ory's Sunshine Orchestra's 1921 recording then entitled *Ory's Creole Trombone*.

The Development of Elemental Jazz

From all of the above it seems possible to draw some conclusions relevant to the earliest stage of development of Elemental Jazz. During a developmental period of some twenty years beginning in the middle of the last decade of the 19th century popular dance music in New Orleans evolved beginning with the application of syncopation to popular songs and dances.

After 1897 Classical ragtime emerged, at a time when street songs and blues were being lifted into the dance halls. By 1900 Buddy Bolden's band was recognised as having created a new dance music style called syncopation or swing music, later called jazz.

Our experiments with the instrumentation, repertoire and performance practices attributed to these early performers reveal a consistent style far from the staid sounds of conventional orchestras of the time. It was not a monolithic style but a melodic style not too remote from much of the jazz of the early recorded era, though without some of the features of the Classic Jazz of King Oliver or the revivalist jazz of Bunk Johnson. It was a time before the Fox trot and the 'toddle time' rhythm, before the barnyard squeals of the ODJB[176] and before the intricate

---

176 Original Dixieland Jazz Band

'improvised' solos of Louis Armstrong, but they were its descendents in the third generation. Much was to change in the ten years before 1927.

Chapter 10

The Heritage of Elemental Jazz

> "... ethno musicologists accepted that the field recordings they made were historically accurate if they could demonstrate that the musical tradition had been handed down from master to apprentice, provided other intervening musical influences had not changed the culture."
>
> —Frank Tirro[177]

What we now call jazz came into being in the mid 1890's in the neighbourhood dance halls of New Orleans though the word jazz did not come into the public consciousness until 1916*. It derived from the vernacular music of the streets but soon both Creole and Uptown black dance musicians were introducing it to dance audiences.

The dance music of Buddy Bolden and his first contemporaries at the beginning of the 20th century comprised simple syncopated tunes played by an improvising ensemble. However this was a significant evolution in popular music.

In an interview with Alan Lomax the clarinettist Alphonse Picou told of his first encounter with the new method before 1900:

> "One day Boul Boul Augustat, the trombone player, heard me practising at the house and ask me if I want

---

177 Tirro F. "Jazz a History" 1993 p 123
* One writer suggested that the word came from the Mandingo word 'jasi' which meant "to act out of the ordinary"(—Mary Cable 1980 p202,) and jazz historian Al Rose said that the word was widely used in New Orleans before 1916 to describe the sexual act

to come to one of his rehearsals. I say, 'You got any music?'

'You don't need no music,' say Boul Boul.

'That's impossible. What am I gonna play? Just sit there and hold my instrument?' I ask.

'Don't worry. You'll know.' That's what Boul Boul tell me."

"So I went. They were playing some good jazz that I didn't know nothing about ... (quotes lyric of *Moi pas l'aimez ça*)

"Well, I had good brains at that time and I caught on quick. When Boul Boul heard me filling in, he say, 'See you know how to play without music.' So I played with Boul Boul's string band then." [178,179]

Picou's initial reaction was a reflection of the considerable change that was occurring. Mark Katz described it thus:

"In jazz, the values of the classical world are inverted: the performance is the primary text, while the score is merely an interpretation."[180]

It is not surprising that there were mixed reactions to the innovation. In another interview Picou said:

---

178 Lomax A. "Mister Jelly Roll" p72

179 There is a lot of confusion about Boul Boul Augustat. On another occasion Picou nominated Boul Boul Fortunea as leader of the first band he played with. To add to the confusion Brian Wood points out that: "It is generally accepted that Picou started with Boulboul Valentin, so Augustat was possibly his given name, which further illustrates the perils of oral history."

To compound the confusion further Picou told John Reid that Boo Boo (sic) Fortunea was the manager of the Independence Orchestra, a role also normally associated with Boul Boul Valentin. It seems reasonable to assume that all these references refer to the same man, though on one occasion Picou said Fortunea played slide trombone while Valentin was known as a valve trombonist.

180 Katz M. "*Capturing Sound—How Technology has Changed Music*" University of California Press Berkeley 2004—Katz goes on to demonstrate the significant influence that sound recording has had on jazz history. For many historians the recordings became the primary texts and many musicians learned to play jazz from listening to old recordings.

"That particular style of playing without music was very new to me. I think it was impossible to me! It seemed a sort of style of playing without notes."[181]

The First Generation

The first generation of bands—those playing before 1900 were a mixed bunch. This was to be expected with the new music at such an early stage. Like Picou they were, at first, not sure how to handle the change of style, and had to work out their own system. Picou said that when they got a new piece of music they would get the music and play the tunes with the music, then after that "we didn't need the music no more."

Early bands (like the Independence Orchestra, and the Clem Brothers Orchestra) adopted the free improvising style and became hotter. After 1905 the Golden Rule Band was considered by one witness to be hotter than the Bolden Band.

Audiences too had mixed reactions. Picou said that when playing with Boul Boul's band:

"Every number we played the people just clapped their hands. We had to play them two or three times and that's the way I started with a band."[182]

This was probably at the *Providence Hall* on Liberty St. Picou went on to play regularly with this group that seems to have formed the nucleus of the Independence Orchestra. Picou fashioned his own individual style of performing in the new style.

Bunk Johnson said that white audiences did not take to the new improvised music though it seems that they did eventually do so. By 1905 we begin to hear of white bands like that of violinist Alex (King) Watzke, and the band led by Bill Gallaty in which a young Nick La Rocca began playing. (Watzke is another who claimed to have composed *Tiger Rag* in 1904). Like the black bands they seem to have comprised a mixture of reading musicians and fakers. The evidence suggests that these were groups that were playing popular songs in a syncopated style not unlike that adopted by the contemporary black bands.

---

181 Shapiro and Hentoff op cit p19
182 Shapiro and Hentoff op cit p 26

Improvisation and Elemental Jazz

Almost all early accounts of Elemental Jazz talk of improvisation, yet, as we have seen, some later performers like Johnny De Droit and Nick La Rocca have sought to deny the role of improvisation before 1917. Readers will recall that La Rocca said:

> "And I never heard any numbers that was *improvised or worked on*. If they played a chorus, they may have add a lil'bit flourishes to 'em of their own." (My italics.)

In contrast Richard Collins claimed that the ability to create variations was an essential skill for what he called New Orleans 'Journeymen musicianers' who should be 'expert reading musicians skilled in harmony and variation, also capable teachers.'[183] He then listed a series of forms of variation important in New Orleans music:

- Melodic or thematic
- Tonal changes of pitch
- Contrapuntal
- Harmonic
- Dynamic
- Ornamental
- Changes in meter and tempo
- Rhythmic variations.

A more academic source defined improvisation:

> "Improvise (or extemporise),—to perform according to spontaneous fancy, not from memory or from written copy—though often a performer improvises 'on' (i.e. round about) a given tune.

And variation:

---

[183] He suggested that the musicians of the Bolden band were just such journeymen musicianers.

"—a passage of music intended as a varied version of some 'given passage' ... such variations may diverge only slightly from the 'theme' of the variations, mainly by melodic ornamentation (as in Mozart), but the more recent tendency is to a looser type allowing for a much freer form of composition."[184]

Analysis of the accounts of Elemental Jazz style presented in Chapter 6 indicates that many, if not all, of the forms of variation listed above were present in Elemental Jazz performances, though it is clear that simple melodic variation was a major feature of the style, as compared with the more excursive forms of variation that began towards the end of the Classic Jazz Era around 1927 and the extreme improvisational styles of Modern Jazz.

It seems clear that what La Rocca meant by 'improvised and worked on" was *transformation*. Jelly Roll Morton said he 'transformed' *La Praline* to *Tiger Rag,* and *La Rocca* made the same claim. What they actually did however was to convert the Waltz, Mazurka and Polka themes to four-four time, ragging the melodies and transforming the Quadrille into a fast multi-themed reel. They added their own individual flourishes to the performance. La Rocca appears to have thought this a defining element of jazz and many of the 'compositions' of the Original Dixieland Jazz Band featured this type of transformation. (According to H.O.Brunn their *Barnyard Blues* was based on the theme of *The Holy City*.)

There is not much evidence of this type of transformation in the record of the Elemental Jazz style before 1907, though some of the tunes played by Bolden may indeed have been simple adaptations of earlier folk material, some of which were believed by listeners to have been Bolden's own compositions. There is stronger evidence that this sort of adaptation of Classic Rags and other ragtime era music began in the second decade of jazz.

The idea of spontaneous free improvisation has been something of a holy grail for jazz lovers ever since the first recordings of the ODJB appeared in 1917. La Rocca and his colleagues claimed they knew not a note of music. However in recent years commentators have noted the amount of preparation that went into the recordings of the early Jazz Age.

---

184 Jacobs A. "A New Dictionary of Music" 1958/1974

Jack Stewart, who has devoted much effort to analysing the contribution of La Rocca to early jazz, found a considerable amount of pre-arrangement in the work of the group, Stewart identified many borrowed sources for the ODJB arrangement of *Tiger Rag* and others deny that the records were improvised at all. As Stewart wrote:

> "Many writers have dismissed the music of both La Rocca and Morton as too stiff and raggy and too arranged to qualify as jazz."[185]

Recent commentators have pointed out that early jazz recordings followed written sources more closely than previously thought. Mark Katz quoted work by David Chevan who found that:

> "... in 1924 Louis Armstrong sent a manuscript of his famous *Cornet Chop Suey* to the Copyright Office two years before he recorded the work. The recording, long hailed as a masterpiece of improvisation, is in fact remarkably similar to the copyright deposit."[186]

Katz attributed this tendency to prepare works in advance to the desire to put the best possible performance on the recording.

Stewart wisely suggested that the development of jazz should best be viewed as a process that had occurred over a period of thirty years and that the innovations of La Rocca and Morton, who he believed probably each thought they invented jazz, should best be viewed from the perspective of the beginnings; he called it the ragtime era.

If Collins is right, bands like that of Bolden prepared for performances using at least some written sources and introduced variations in melody and rhythm, depending on their own abilities. Undoubtedly this involved improvisation.

Peter Bocage said of Bolden: "That's the way jazz started just his improvision (sic) ..."

---

185 Stewart J. "The Strangest Bedfellows: Nick La Rocca and Jelly Roll Morton." The Jazz Archivist vol XV 2001 p29
186 Katz M. "Capturing Sound—How Technology Has Changed Music" p75

The Developing Tradition

A number of the early jazz bands that performed in the Bolden Era (1896/1907) appear not to have survived long afterwards. Bolden's band disappeared in 1907 to be replaced by Frank Duson's Eagle Band, playing the same mix of tunes until 1917. Manuel Perez continued playing in a more conventional manner until he left for Chicago in 1915.

However around the end of Bolden's career a number of younger players began to perform.

Fred Keppard who had played street music (violin, mandolin, accordion and guitar) learned cornet from Adolph Alexander who played with the Golden Rule Orchestra. He joined the Olympia Orchestra, then managed by valve trombonist Joe Petit, as star cornetist and began making a name for himself.

Armand Piron, who began playing violin with the Piron-Gaspard Dance Orchestra around 1900, was also to become a major figure in the later development of the music. Jelly Roll Morton, primarily a pianist in New Orleans, claimed he invaded the jazz scene in 1902 and by 1906 he was taking bands to California and elsewhere. Each of these men was, in his own way, to make a considerable contribution to the continuation and later development of the tradition.

After 1900 popular music tastes began to change, the Coon Songs began to disappear; ragtime was the rage throughout the nation. There was a flood of mass produced 'ragtime' songs, though many retained the Coon Song flavour. Nevertheless the old dances remained in vogue. They still played Quadrilles, Waltzes, and Schottisches along with the Ragtime Two-step and romantic love songs. As time went by, changes of style were introduced as the older players disappeared and the newer ones developed their own approach to arrangement and improvisation.

Instrumental Changes

The second decade of jazz saw the introduction of the piano, though many black bands retained a rhythm section consisting of guitar, bowed bass and drums. A major change also occurred with the gradual replacement of the valve trombone by the slide trombone played in the new tailgate style. At some point after 1912 some players began to develop the slap bass style, though the instrument was still often bowed until the early 1920's. White New Orleans bands appear to have dropped the violin after 1910, though black bands continued to use the violin lead until the 1920's.

Changing the Elemental Style

Although it could be said that a consistent style had been developed within the limits set by the abilities of the performers of the first decade there was not a lot of change during the ten years when the Bolden Band was active. It appears reasonable to look further ahead to see how the style was transmitted and how it changed.

Fred Keppard began playing during the last year of Bolden's career. (ca 1906) Some witnesses said he increased the range of variations and took them into the higher part of the cornet's range. He also played more late numbers than Bolden. He became the star attraction of the Olympia Orchestra and headlined it until around 1913.

Bunk Johnson claimed he began playing cornet with the dance Orchestra of Adam Olivier at age 17 (probably around 1905.[187])[188] He claimed to have played with the Bolden Band, and later played with The Original Superior Orchestra and valve trombonist Frank Duson's Eagle Band.

Duson may have played with Bolden before 1900 but by 1906 appears to have been managing the Bolden Band. He continued to lead the Eagle Band until 1917.

Armand Piron who was playing with the Piron-Gaspard Dance Orchestra around 1900 moved, first, to the Peerless Orchestra, and then to the Eagle Band, shortly after the end of Bolden's career. He took over leadership of the Olympia Orchestra when Keppard left town around 1914.

It was players like these who were to form the bridge to carry the music into its second generation. Jelly Roll Morton had left town earlier but was developing his own style of performance elsewhere, using a mixture of local and imported New Orleans musicians; perhaps the first stage of a cultural diffusion that was to see the eventual appearance of jazz on the international arena.

---

[187] The date depends on the date of his birth which has been disputed but 1905 seems reasonable.
[188] It is now believed that this was the band of A.Oleavia or O'leavia see Abbott and Seroff op cit index

New bands entered the scene early in the second decade. The Original Superior Orchestra led by Peter Bocage (ca 1908) began experimenting with Classical Ragtime. The Magnolia Band formed by Louis Keppard introduced Joe 'King' Oliver to New Orleans audiences around the same time.

By and large, noisy brass instruments were not allowed to perform in the Storyville red light district until permission was obtained to admit them to the cabarets in the district around 1907 when Fred Keppard took a novel five-piece band into the cabarets. Jelly Roll Morton called it the first Dixieland Band. To save cost Keppard dropped the violin, guitar and bass and introduced the piano to his rhythm section.

Numerous other cabaret bands of varying sizes flooded into the cabarets, including the Tuxedo Orchestra (ca1910) playing in the large Tuxedo Cabaret. This comprised violin, cornet, slide trombone, clarinet, piccolo, bass violin, drums and piano. A newspaper report said the Tuxedo Band played the latest in popular music and some compositions of their own.

Some time after 1908, out of town valve trombonist Edward Kid Ory, who had brought his band to New Orleans acquired a slide trombone and began developing a new style later called 'gut-bucket' or 'tailgate trombone'. This style was further developed by Jack Carey who was playing in the Allen Brass Band around 1910.

Fig.17 Above (left) Jack Carey and Kid Ory (right) inventors of the 'tailgate' trombone style

By 1913 Ory's Band and Carey's Crescent Band were the 'hot ticket' bands playing a rough free interpretation of ragtime. By 1917 the Ory-Oliver band, a group derived from Piron's Olympia Orchestra provided a springboard from which black musicians were to take their music North and East.

White bands appeared in the record after 1905 and there appears to have been a consistent development of style in Jack Laine's bands and in others like Bill Gallaty's High Rollers (1908), Violinist Ernest Giardina's Tonti Social Club Band (1908), Frank Christian's Band (1910), Happy Schilling's Band (1910) and Abbie Brunies' Band 1911.

It was in these bands that the musicians who were to take white jazz to Chicago and create the first recorded jazz developed their skills.

Tom Brown's Band from Dixieland formed in 1913 went North in 1915. Brown claimed his was the first band to be called a jazz (jass) band.

In 1913 the nucleus of Johnny Stein's Band was playing in the 102 Club in Storyville. That band went North in 1916 and eventually reformed to become the Original Dixieland Jazz Band.

The second decade was also to see the publication of many of the tunes that were to become jazz standards; tunes like *That's Aplenty, Some Of These Days, Très Moutarde,* W.Tyer's *Panama,*—and *Dallas Blues.* The years after 1910 also saw the transformation of many ragtime tunes into jazz standards by bands like Jack Carey's Crescent Jazz Band and eventually the ODJB.

Fig.18 Above: The Original Creole Orchestra. Note that, apart from the slide trombone, the band retains the old violin led instrumentation.

That Famous Creole (Ragtime) Orchestra

Around 1914 Jelly Roll Morton's brother in law, bassist Bill Johnson had a band in California that included New Orleans violinist Jimmy Palao and he reinforced it by sending to New Orleans for the front line of Fred Keppard's "Dixieland Band"—musicians drawn from the Olympia Orchestra, including Freddie, clarinettist George Baquet and trombonist Eddie Vincent.[189] To this he added Norwood Williams, guitar and Dink Johnson traps.

They played jobs around Los Angeles until they attracted the attention of the owner of the Pantages theatre chain and were launched on a stage career touring the vaudeville circuits. The band that appeared on the stage did not include the drummer, but worked with a black-faced singer, performing a plantation scene that included a hokum chicken act as well as playing 'ragtime' tunes and old favourites like *Swanee River* and *Old Black Joe*.[190]

The group toured many cities to considerable acclaim until it finally broke up in 1918. Reports indicate that the band was very strong musically. Jelly Roll Morton said:

> "The Creole Band was *tremendous*. They really played *jazz*, not just novelty and show stuff."

The significance of the Original Creole Orchestra is that it was taking the early New Orleans style to a wide national audience before the first recordings appeared in 1917. The core of the group were musicians who had performed during the latter stages of Bolden's career; Jimmy Palao leading the Imperial Orchestra, Keppard, Baquet and Eddie Vincent in the Olympia Orchestra. It was thus a direct link with bands of the Bolden Era.

Links in the Chain[191]

It will be seen from Chart 2 that the direct influence of the musicians of Buddy Bolden's Band did not survive into the recording age.

---

189 Vincent had by that time abandoned the valve trombone for a slide instrument.
190 The act is well described in Gushee L. "Pioneers of Jazz" pp106ff
191 What follows is a summation of an account presented in considerably more detail in the Author's "Exploring Early Jazz—The Origins and Evolution of the New Orleans Style" 2002

The aura of the Eagle Band may have made itself felt in the Olympia Orchestra through the Eagle Band's former leader, Armand Piron, when he took over leadership of the Olympia in 1914, but new influences were brought to bear in that band from musicians, who may have heard Bolden, but had learned the style elsewhere; King Oliver in the Rozelle Band, Kid Ory in his own band. These men formed the seminal Ory/Oliver Band around 1917 leading to the classic black jazz recordings of the early twenties. Piron too went on to record with his own group that contained a number of musicians from the Bolden Era. His recordings provide the only recorded examples of the early New Orleans violinist leader in action.

Fred Keppard left the Original Creole Orchestra in 1918 at the end of its successful stage career and went on to perform in the North throughout the early twenties. His individual style of playing passed into the recorded heritage in numerous recordings with commercial bands and with his own band in 1926. One record reviewer described him in these recordings as 'an earlier stylist adrift in the jazz age sounds of Chicago'. Perhaps we are hearing in those recordings the sound of the man witnesses said sounded most like Buddy Bolden.

White bands appear to have developed in a separate stream beginning with the Jack Laine brass bands, but it is difficult to identify any concrete influences before 1903 when bands were formed that influenced the development of players later to form part of the first recorded band. After 1921 the recording became a major medium for dissemination of black and white jazz alike.

Passing On The Heritage

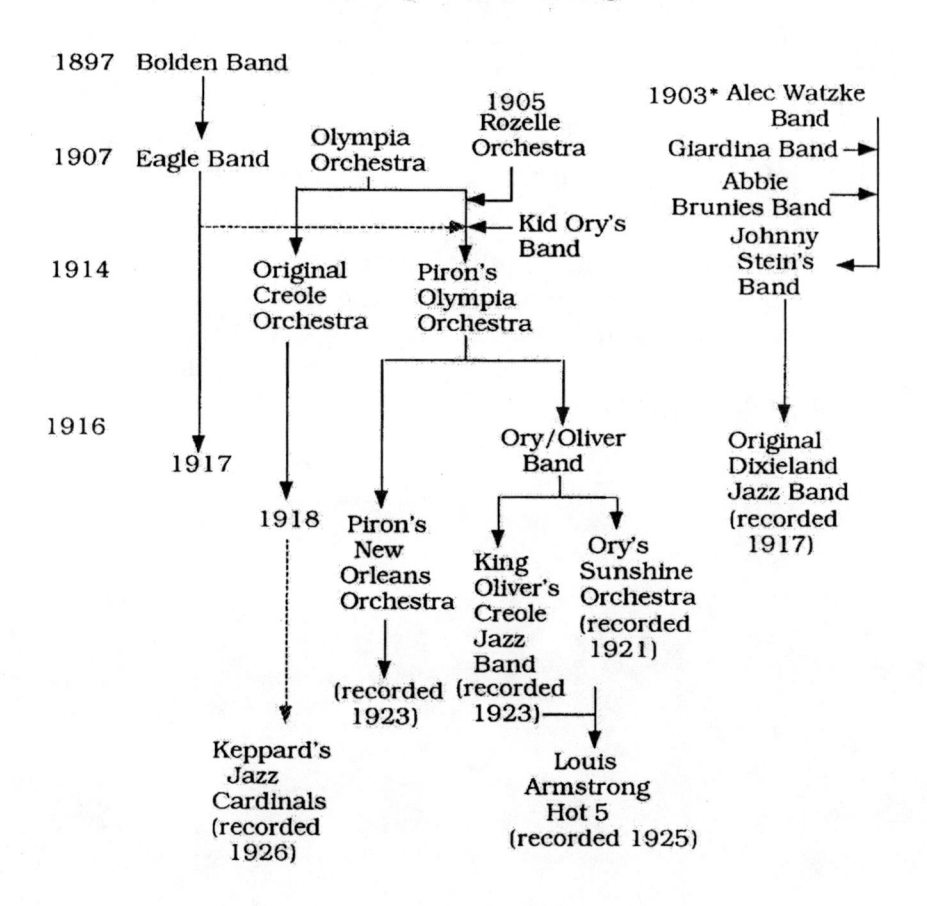

1897 Bolden Band
1907 Eagle Band — Olympia Orchestra
1905 Rozelle Orchestra
1903* Alec Watzke Band
Giardina Band →
Abbie Brunies Band
Kid Ory's Band
Johnny Stein's Band
1914 Original Creole Orchestra — Piron's Olympia Orchestra
1916
1917
Ory/Oliver Band
Original Dixieland Jazz Band (recorded 1917)
1918 Piron's New Orleans Orchestra
King Oliver's Creole Jazz Band
Ory's Sunshine Orchestra (recorded 1921)
(recorded 1923) (recorded 1923)
Keppard's Jazz Cardinals (recorded 1926)
Louis Armstrong Hot 5 (recorded 1925)

Chart 2 Above: Passing On The Heritage

Jazz began in 1890's in response to a desire for syncopated music that was already part of an earlier black music tradition. It appeared in the street songs of New Orleans and in the broken rhythms of popular Coon Songs, cakewalks and minstrel songs published in that decade. By 1917 what was a simple formula of melody dominated improvisation had been changed by interaction with classical ragtime compositions, new dances, and changing instrumentation, and it was beginning to show the features of what was to become the Classic Jazz of the early 1920's.

Our experiment with the repertoire, instrumentation and performance practices described by witnesses to the music of Buddy Bolden and his contemporaries reveals a sound that it is recognisably jazz; not too different from the earliest recordings if not quite as structured and frenetic.

What was called syncopation or swing in the 1890's changed its name with fashions popular music. In an interview in the 1940's Bunk Johnson Bunk Johnson said:

> "They had years ago ragtime, and the later years they changed it to jazz. Now the later the years have gotten they changed it to swing and it's going back to jazz, and back to jazz it's going back right on home to ragtime. It's gonna be right on where we started.

Chapter 11

Revivals in Retrospect

"Anyone who heard him in his comeback years never really heard Bunk. You should have heard him as a young colt. Wonderful."

—Big Boy Goudie[192]

Jazz critics, journalists and record collectors only became interested in the authentic sound and style of the earliest jazz around 1940. In that year Heywood Hale Broun got together a number of old musicians some of whom had been around before 1900 and recorded some jazz standards in the hope of recreating the sound of early jazz.

There was immediate controversy about these performances. Some authorities thought they were tapping a vein of authentic sound, others were appalled at the apparent discordance and limited musical technique displayed. Some could not believe that the hot jazz of the early 1920's could have emerged from such roots.

Doug Landau recently commented of the Hale Broun session:

> ... "while not quite the equivalent of John Hanning Speke's discovery of the Nile, it marked the first tangible outcome of what might be dubbed 'Jazz Archaeology'."[193]

---

192 quoted in Landau D. "Wooden Joe Nicholas—a Genesis Echo?" New Orleans Music Vol 11 No1 p18

193 Landau D. "Wooden Joe Nicholas—a Genesis Echo?" New Orleans Music Vol 11 No1 p14 (The title of the article reminds us that Wooden Joe Nicholas of whom he writes was there at the beginning.)

I found in a dictionary the following definition of Archaeology:

> "—the scientific study of any culture, esp. a prehistoric one, by excavation and description of its remains."

In Exploring *Early Jazz: The Origins and Evolution of the New Orleans Style"* I lamented the relative lack of interest in Jazz Historiography and the partial and inaccurate works of many jazz writers. Recently, serious historians like Jack Stewart[194] and Lawrence Gushee have remarked on the lack of a factually grounded discourse on jazz. In the introduction to his own thoroughly researched history of the Creole band Gushee comments that:

> "... in serious writings about jazz, discography has been primary, bibliography distinctly secondary, to the point that one suspects that an enduring tradition of writing on jazz is to downplay the importance of both primary published documents and the work of other writers."[195]

He also commented on an over emphasis in the literature on the style of playing of "certain classic recordings" of the period 1923–1928. By those standards the 1940 recordings of Kid Rena's Delta Jazz Band sound primitive indeed. However from our point of view that is not the comparison that matters. Any evaluation of the Kid Rena performances should rather be aimed at establishing to what extent they really do represent the music of the Bolden Era. In the absence of recorded data, the primary sources (including Oral History), along with bibliographic sources, including biographies and auto-biographies, need to be rigorously examined for information on instrumentation, performance practices and repertoire. This process formed the basis for our own reconstruction of Elemental Jazz.

In the years following the Hale Broun experiment increasing attention was paid to the music of older surviving jazzman like Bunk Johnson and George Lewis. It was recorded and became the basis for what was called the New Orleans Revival. This music sounded very different from the recorded classic jazz of the 1920's and it was assumed by many that it represented a genuine return to the roots of the New Orleans Style. It was emulated by younger musicians, particularly groups in England and Europe and still forms the basis for what its aficionados call the

---

194 Stewart J. Jazz Archivist vol ix p23
195 Gushee L. op cit p155

New Orleans Style. Significantly, when the Hale Broun recordings were issued on CD it was under the title "Prelude to the Revival Vol II"[196].

What They Played

Following our review of the Bolden repertoire it seems reasonable to look again at the list of compositions recorded by Kid Rena's Delta Jazz Band in 1940. They were:

> Panama (W. Tyers) 1911
> High Society (Steele) 1903
> Gettysburg March (Stambaugh) 1911
> Milneberg Joys (Morton) 1923/1925[197]
> Clarinet Marmalade (La Rocca/ODJB) 1918
> Weary Blues (Matthews) 1915
> Low Down Blues
> Get It Right

Of the first six tunes on the list only *High Society* was published during the Bolden Era, though it did not appear in my original list of Bolden's tunes. They are more representative of the tunes published during the careers of the second generation of jazz bands and, with the possible exception of *Gettysburg March*, belong to what has been called the canon of Dixieland jazz standards. The *Lowdown Blues* is a traditional improvised 12 bar blues. *Get It Right* appears to be based on the same melody as Kid Ory's *Do What Ory Say*, and may be an earlier traditional version. (According to Brian Wood, Albert Nicholas is reported to have said that Ory did not write *Do What Ory Say*, it was an old family tune everyone knew as "K.M.F.A".)

This choice of repertoire clearly reflects a later stage of development of early jazz than the Elemental Jazz of Bolden's time, pushing into the beginning of the recorded era after 1917. In this respect, the recordings reflect the more complex style of head arrangements developed by Kid Ory, Jack Carey and others around 1913. A number of the tunes were widely performed during the Classic Jazz era of the 1920's and were well known in 1940, thus inviting comparison with recorded performances by the jazz masters of the roaring 20's. There are no ragtime

---

196 American Music CD AMCD 41
197 First recorded 1923 but not copyrighted until 1925

Coon Songs or popular love songs, no rags and no conventional dance compositions. Only one blues appears, and only *Get it Right* might be a traditional vernacular dance song. The musicians appear to have chosen routines they had become familiar with between 1911 and 1940.

The Instrumentalists

Superficially the instrumentation of Kid Rena's jazz band appears to mirror that shown in the only photograph of Buddy Bolden's band, with the addition of a trap drummer. However, it also shows influences from the Jazz Age. Significantly Rena plays trumpet, not cornet, as did most of the horn players during the ensuing New Orleans Revival. Although one or two bands during Bolden's time had a slide trombonist the majority employed the valve instrument. In these recordings the slide trombone is preferred, and the record cover suggests Albert Glenny plays slap bass not bowed bass. Two clarinet players were employed using simple system clarinets. Apart from the use of the second clarinet and the absence of a piano this combination might have seemed more normal in 1940 than in Bolden's time. In particular, though Bolden did use the clarinet lead at times, more often he and his competitors had a violinist leader.

The musicians themselves are interesting. Specifically they were:

>Henry Kid Rena born 1898 Trumpet
>Alphonse Picou born 1878 Clarinet
>Louis "Big Eye" Nelson (de Lille) born 1885 Clarinet
>Jim Robinson born 1892 Slide Trombone
>Joe Rena Born 1897 Drums
>Willie Santiago born 1887 Guitar
>Albert Gleny (Glenny) born 1870 String Bass

Of these musicians Picou (28), Nelson (21), Santiago (19) and Gleny (36) were active musicians when Bolden left the scene in 1906. Robinson (14) who came from Deer Park Plantation (near Point La Hache) could have heard the Bolden band had he then been in New Orleans but this is uncertain. The Rena brothers, Henry (8) and Joe (9) respectively, were probably too young to have formed a clear impression of Bolden's music. Picou is known to have been active throughout the second half of the 1890's and Nelson claimed to have been playing with Bolden in 1900 during the Robert Charles riots. Glenny (see fig.6 Chapter 3) was somewhat older than Bolden and is known to have played with the Bolden band. He is known to have then played a 3 string bass and preferred playing with the bow.[198] Kid Rena had a good reputation as a trumpet player bandleader in the early 1920's and Peter Bocage compared his playing favourably with that of Bolden.[199] On balance, these musicians would appear to have had the background to recreate the early jazz style.

How They Played

Listening to these recordings again after our experiment with recreation they do appear in some ways to reflect the sound of original jazz. In particular the heavy emphasis on melody, in ensemble and in solos, is consistent with what we have learned of the Elemental Style. However, musicians in earlier bands were known to continue performing behind other players who were handed the lead. This is largely absent in the Rena recordings, possibly because the players had become accustomed to take down when performing during the intervening Jazz Age and Swing Era. The clarinet solos were usually simple embellishments of the melody except when performing the set piece *High Society* clarinet choruses. This too is consistent with the evidence about early jazz The trombone played vamping trombone in most ensemble passages with occasional tailgate glissandi but when handed the lead improvised in a free manner much more typical of the style of the Jazz Age than that of 1906.

Multi themed works like *Clarinet Marmalade* were performed much as they would have been by bands from 1917 onwards, though in a much less aggressive manner. Strangely they played only one theme of Morton's *Milneberg Joys* repeating it endlessly, probably as might have been done by a 'chorus band' of the early 20th Century. However their performance the simpler *Get It Right* also played in 'chorus band' style might be as close as they got to the beginnings of jazz—all ensemble no solos.

I found it difficult to evaluate the only blues on the session—(*Low Down Blues*). It sounded much like other blues recorded during the 34 years that had intervened since the end of Bolden's career by bands

---

198 Wood B. "The Song for Me" bio entry for Gleny
199 HJA interview 1959

as diverse as those of Muggsy Spanier and Jimmy Noone, and later recordings by bands like those of Bunk Johnson and Kid Ory. Maybe this approach does reflect the early instrumental blues tradition handed down in an unbroken chain through the second and third generations of jazz musicians.

The performances were resolutely four-beat, except for a few choruses in which the drummer emphasised the second and third beats. Accordingly this cannot be regarded as typical of Elemental Jazz. On the other hand, the light but propulsive sound of the rhythm section mirrored our own experience.

Overall, while the music of Rena's Delta jazz Band does contain elements imported from jazz of later periods it has a primitive sound that is probably authentic. Occasional discords occur, particularly among the clarinettists competing for space. Some writers felt that this may have been typical of early jazz. Edmond Souchon wrote that early performances by King Oliver (ca 1907) were rough and contained many bad notes but said he preferred them to later performances by Oliver when he had smoothed out his style.[200] Of course we found from our own experience it's easy to make the odd error and that was probably true in Bolden's time.

These early recording did provide for the first time an indication of the styles of two of the earliest jazz clarinettists, in itself a major find for the jazz archaeologist.

The Revival Revisited

The analysis above raises similar questions about the revivalist movement that followed. For reasons that are not clear, the major bands of the revival era did not seek to revive the instrumentation of the earliest jazz bands. In general they mimicked the composition of Classic Jazz groups—a format that appears to have derived from that of the Original Dixieland Jazz Band; three front line, trumpet, clarinet and slide trombone, piano and drums, increasingly augmented with banjo and slap bass. Only one violinist, Peter Bocage, made a very few recordings during the Revival, and he was often asked by listeners why he continued to play the violin, which they then considered an inappropriate inclusion in a jazz band. Bocage apparently replied that he

---

200 in Gottlieb R. ed "Reading Jazz" Pantheon NY 1996 p345

knew more about jazz than did the aficionados. In bands of the revival era the trumpet played lead.

The repertoire of the revival was dominated by jazz standards like that of the Rena recordings, though a number of the Bolden Era favourites like *Make Me a Pallet on the Floor*, *My Bucket's Got a Hole In It* and *Any Rags* re-emerged. In general Coon Songs were not performed. Some few classic rags reappeared in rough arrangements as did some turn of the century sentimental songs. However Bunk Johnson contended that more contemporary popular songs should have been performed and he received some criticism for that. In his last recording date he did include examples of hit tunes of the day. Creole tunes that were not listed by witnesses to the Bolden repertoire, reappeared. Sentimental low down blues performances were commonplace.

In the general, although Bunk Johnson himself played in the Bolden era most of the musicians of the so-called New Orleans Revival were younger players, like George Lewis (born 1900), whose musical styles were emulated by many younger musicians. These players had developed their styles influenced by music in the city during the 1920's and 1930's. They did not play like the stars of the New Orleans Diaspora who found employment in Northern cities and were recorded in the 1920's. In 1940 many of those Northern based players were performing in a style increasingly influenced by 1930's swing. It cannot be said however that the performances of the down home revivalists derived directly from jazz of the Bolden Era as there were evident in them features like the trumpet lead, full chorus solos and four beat rhythm that only appeared after 1917.

Kid Ory's Creole Jazz Band that recorded in the early 1940's is an interesting touchstone. Witnesses aver that Ory played in 1940 largely as he did 1917 and a direct comparison can be made with his recordings of 1921. The Ory band of 1940 played much faster than his band of 1921, but when that is taken into account, its composition and general style were not too different from some those of the revival bands. In 1917, after hearing the ODJB recordings, Ory dropped the violin lead and introduced the piano. This suggests that the revivalist bands may really represent a survival of a style played in New Orleans at the end of the second decade of jazz, and in the 1920's (after the abandonment of the violin lead, and before the widespread introduction of the saxophone) probably by groups like the unrecorded bands of Chris Kelly and Buddy Petit.

They were, in instrumentation, closer to the ODJB than that of the Oliver Creole Jazz Band, though they played in a looser more laid back style than either. This may be attributed to the major influence of Bunk Johnson who played in a very laid back style. Johnson showed glimpses of a strong technique and creative improvisational ability. However his playing was sometimes flawed and erratic. Witnesses described his performances in the Bolden Era as more assured and subtle. We do, however get from his recordings, a window through which to glimpse the authentic sound of early jazz. It would have been interesting to hear him playing the cornet.

Other Revival Traditions

Traditional jazz players not born in the United States often followed the revivalist school, but a significant proportion of American bands drew their influences from elsewhere. The majority appear to have been influenced by the school of Northern white players who continued to play traditional jazz throughout the years when Swing and Be bop dominated jazz recordings. They draw inspiration from the white bands of Eddie Condon and his colleagues who performed during the Chicago jazz boom of the 1920's and later transferred to New York. Numerous United States bands follow this style today. Its roots lie in the music of the ODJB, the New Orleans Rhythm Kings and the Wolverine Orchestra in the early 1920's. In passing it absorbed influences from Swing and what was later called later Mainstream jazz. It was largely uninfluenced by the New Orleans revival. These players see themselves as following the genuine Dixieland tradition with which they grew up. And it is so.

What differentiates this style from jazz of the Bolden era are features like the very fast tempi introduced by the ODJB, the extravagant solos of the swing era; use of the trumpet, slide trombone, tenor saxophone and slap bass. Some employ guitar, others the five string or tenor banjos.

Another group of United States musicians of the 1940's drew their inspiration from black bands recorded in the North during the 1920's, in particular from the recordings of King Oliver's Creole Jazz Band made in 1923. This East Coast Revival which began with Lu Watters Yerba Buena Jazz Band in California had a significant influence in the United States and elsewhere. A number of American traditional jazz bands continue to perform in this tradition. A glance at Chart 2 Chapter10 will reveal that this group was indeed following in a tradition derived from New Orleans in the 1920's. Many changes had occurred by 1920.

A Window to the Past

Though they are by no means experiments in revivalism the recordings made by Armand Piron's New Orleans Orchestra beginning in 1923, (made around the same time as the first classic recordings of King Oliver's Creole Jazz Band,) provide another glimpse of the early jazz style, and it is interesting to subject them to comparison with the criteria of performance established for Elemental Jazz as indicated in a previous chapter. This was an orchestra that had a direct line of descent from the original Olympia Orchestra that was formed in Bolden's time. (See Chart 2 Chapter 10). In 1923 it had Piron on violin and leader. Its trumpet player was Peter Bocage, former leader of the Original Superior Orchestra who learned cornet from Bunk Johnson around 1910. Drummer Louis Cottrell(e) played with John Robichaux and Keppard's Olympia Orchestra. Clarinettist Lorenzo Tio (born 1893) was playing in the Onward Brass Band around 1910. These players had very personal links with the Bolden Era.

Unfortunately Piron had picked up the habit of including saxophones in his line up, but that being taken out of the equation, the combination of the violin with the three horn front line remains to be observed, particularly in a 1923 version of *West Indies Blues* made with singer Esther Bigeou.

Gushee lamented the neglect of the important work of the Original Creole Orchestra, a neglect he has now remedied. However the many recordings of the Piron Orchestra have suffered similar neglect. Geoff Bull has suggested that the group made further recordings under the name of Charles Matson and this would seem to be a fruitful field for research. Perhaps a future researcher might be persuaded turn his/her attention to telling the story of Piron and his extensive contributions to the history of early jazz.

Critical Differences

The New Orleans Revivalists sought to go back further into the roots of the music. However insufficient attention was paid to significant evidence about the instrumentation, repertoire and performance practices of the Elemental Jazz period. Consequently though the style retains a number of features retained from the Bolden Era, it also features elements from later periods. It has to be said that the differences are not great. However the addition of the violin, cornet and valve trombone does make a significant change to the overall sound, as does adherence to the two beat rhythm. Some tunes like *Don't Go Way Nobody* which were played in the Revival period had clearly suffered modification over time. Performances based on original score material are more raggy and in some respects hotter. They are probably truer to the period in which they were composed—the time when jazz was born.

From the historian's point of view these differences are important. From the data in Chapter 6 it is possible to develop a set of guidelines that can be used to evaluate the success of attempts to recreate the music of a given era. Thus it is possible to hear in Humphrey Lyttleton's 1986 BBC recordings[201] a genuine attempt to recreate the sound of the two-clarinet Bolden Band ca 1905. Similarly we can evaluate the Imperial Serenaders recordings of 1999[202] on which period performances of the 3/4 component of music of the Bolden Era repertoire were included. Neither includes the violin lead, and each, in some respects, falls short of an ideal application of the research findings.[203]

Readers wishing to hear how a New Orleans Revival Era band might sound playing the Bolden repertoire would surely enjoy the Gota River Jazzmen's 2003 CD "... Thought I heard Buddy Bolden Play"[204]. It is a typical European Revivalist group that had no pretension to recording authentic performances, intending only to present its own version of some of the tunes Buddy played. Surely, if the unconscious assumptions of the 1940's revivalists had been correct, this would have been how Buddy's band sounded, but those were inadequate assumptions.

There may be more to learn from the archives and other sources about the bands of the Elemental Jazz period, their composition, repertoire and performance styles. If new material does come to light our Archaeologists model of the style may have to be adjusted to take account of them. In the meantime we propose to continue to refine our

---

201 "Gonna Call My Children Home—Music of Buddy Bolden" Calligraph LP CLGLP01
202 "Music of the Bolden Era" Stomp Off CD 1351CD
203 More detailed comments on these recreations appear in the author's "Exploring Early Jazz: The Origins and Evolution Of the New Orleans Style" pp287/295
204 "... Thought I Heard Buddy Bolden Play" GRJCD06

approach to performing music from the Bolden Era and take it to the jazz audience.

Bibliography

Abbott Lynn and Seroff D. "Out Of Sight: the Rise of African American Popular Music" 2002 University Press of Mississippi, Jackson.

Allen W.F. Ware C.P. W. McKim-Garrison Lucy 1867 "Slave Songs of the United States", A.G Simpson &Co., New York

Asbury H. "The French Quarter" 1936/1964 Mockingbird Books, St Simons Island Ga.

Barker D. "Bourbon St. Black" 1973 Oxford University Press, New York

Berlin E.A. "Reflections and Research on Ragtime', I.S.A.M. Monographs No 24 1987 Brooklyn College, New York

Berlin E.A. "King Of Ragtime—Scott Joplin and His Era", 1995 Oxford University Press New York

Berlin E.A. "Ragtime a Musical and Cultural History", 1980 University of California Press, Berkeley

Blassingame J.W. "Black New Orleans 1860-1880", 1973 University of Chicago Press, Chicago

Blesh R. "Shining Trumpets", 1946/1954 Cassel & Co, London

Blesh R. and Janis "They all Played Ragtime", 1950 Knopf, New York

Cable Mary "Lost New Orleans" 1980 Houghton Mifflin Books, Boston

Collins R. "New Orleans Jazz a Revised History", 1996 Vantage Press, New York

Davies N. "Europe East and West" 2006 Johnathon Cape London

Dodds W. (Baby) and Gara L. "The Baby Dodds Story" Louisiana State University Press, Baton Rouge, 1959/92

Dominguez V.R. "White by Definition" 1986 Rutgers University Press, New Brunswick NJ.

Elson J. "History of American Music" 1925 MacMillan, New York.

Epstein Dena J. "Sinful Tunes and Spirituals: Black Folk Music to the Civil War", 1977 University of Illinois Press, Urbana.

Evans Oliver "New Orleans" 1959 Macmillan, New York.

Ewen David "Panorama of American Popular Music", 1957 Prentice Hall, Englewood Cliffs, New Jersey.

Foster P. "Pops Foster"1971 University of California Press Berkeley.

Gottlieb R. ed "Reading Jazz" 1996 Pantheon NY

Grossman W. And Farrel J "The Heart Of Jazz" 1956 New York University Press, New York.

Gushee L. "Pioneers of Jazz: The Story of the Creole Band" 2005 Oxford University Press NY

Gushee L. "The Nineteenth Century Origins of Jazz" 1994 Black Music Research Journal (BMRJ) Vol 14 No1 pp1-24

Hall-Quest Olga "Old New Orleans, the Creole City its role in American History 1718/1803" 1968 Dutton, New York.

Handy W.C. "Father Of the Blues", 1957 Sidgwick and Jackson London.

Hardie D. "The Ancestry of Jazz: A Musical Family History" 2004 iUniverse Lincoln Nebraska

Hardie D. "The Loudest Trumpet: Buddy Bolden and the Early History of Jazz", 2000 toExcel, Lincoln Nebraska.

Hardie D. "Exploring Early Jazz: The Origins and Evolution of the New Orleans Style", 2002 Writer's Club Press, Lincoln, Nebraska.

Hasse J. E. Ed. "Ragtime Its History Composers and Music", 1985 MacMillan Press London.

Hitchcock H.W. "Music in the United States" 1969 Prentice—Hall, Englewood Cliffs New Jersey.

Jacobs A. "A New Dictionary of Music" 1958/1974 Penguin Middlesex

Jasen D. and Tichenor T. "Rags and Ragtime, A Musical History", 1978 The Seabury Press, New York.

Jasen D. and Jones G. "Spreadin the Rhythm Around; Black Popular Songwriters 1880/1930" 1998 Schirmer Books, New York.

Katz M. Capturing Sound—How Technology has Changed Music 2004 University of California Press Berkeley

Kingman D. "American Music a Panorama", 1979/1990 Schirmer Books, New York

Koenig K. "Louisiana Brass Bands and History in Relation to Jazz History", 1983 The Second Line Vol xxxv Summer 1983, New Orleans.

Lloyd Tanya "New Orleans" 2001 Whitecap Books, Vancouver.

Lomax Alan "Mr Jelly Roll", 1952 Cassell and Company London.

Lomax Alan "The Land Where the Blues Began" 1994 Methuen London.

Lomax John and Lomax Alan "Beloved American Folk Songs" 1947 Grosset and Dunlap, New York.

Marquis D. "In Search of Buddy Bolden-First Man of Jazz" 1978/1993 Louisiana State University Press, Baton Rouge.

Marsalis W. "Marsalis On Music" 1995 Norton, New York.

Mitchell W.R. "Classic New Orleans" 1993 Martin-St Martin Publishing, University of Georgia Press, Athens Ga.

Muse Vance "Old New Orleans", 1988 Rebus Inc., Birmingham Al.

Morgan T.L. and Barlow W. "From Cakewalks to Concert Halls: An Illustrated History of African American Popular Music from 1895 to1930" 1992 Elliott & Clark, Washington DC

Parrish Lydia "Slave Songs Of the Georgia Sea Islands" 1942/1992 University of Georgia Press.

Ramsey F. et al "Jazzmen" 1939 Harcourt Brace, NY

Roberts J.S "The Latin Tinge—the Impact of Latin American Music on The United States" 1979/1999 Oxford University Press, NY

Roberts J.S. "Latin Jazz" 1999 Schirmer Books, NY

Roberts J.S. "Black Music of Two Worlds" 2nd ed 1998 Schirmer Books NY

Rose A. and Souchon E. "New Orleans Jazz—A Family Album" 1967 Louisiana State University Press, Baton Rouge.

Russel W. "New Orleans Style" 1994 Jazzology Press New Orleans

Saxon L. "Fabulous New Orleans" 1928/1998 Pelican Publishing New Orleans.

Sandjeck R. "America's Popular Music and its Business", 1988 Oxford University Press, New York.

Schafer W.J. and Riedel J. "The Art of Ragtime", 1973/1977 reprint Da Capo, New York.

Schuller G. "Early Jazz", 1968 Oxford University Press, New York.

Searight Sara "New Orleans" 1973 Stein and Day, New York.

Southern E. "The Music of Black Americans"1971/1997 Norton, New York.

Spaeth S. "History of Popular Music in America"1948 Random House New York.

Stewart J. "Cuban Influences On New Orleans Music" Essay published with CD 7032 "The Cuban Danzón—Before There Was Jazz—1906 to 1929"

Stewart J. "Cuban Influences on New Orleans Music" The Jazz Archivist Vol xiii (1998-1999) Hogan Jazz Archive Tulane University, New Orleans.

Stewart J. "The Mexican Band Legend—Part II" The Jazz Archivist Vol ix (May 1990) Hogan Jazz Archive Tulane University, New Orleans.

Stewart J. "The Original Dixieland Jazz Band's Place in the Development of Jazz" The Jazz Archivist Vol xix (2005/6) p16 Hogan Jazz Archive Tulane University, New Orleans

Stewart J. "The Strangest of Bedfellows: Nick La Rocca and Jelly Roll Morton" The Jazz Archivist Vol xv (2001) p23 Hogan Jazz Archive Tulane University, New Orleans.

Tirro F. "Jazz a History" Norton NY 1993 p 123

Turner F "Remembering Song"1982/1994 Da Capo, New York.

Van der Merwe Peter "Origins of the Popular Style"1989/1992 Clarendon Press Oxford.

Wilder Alex. "American Popular Song 1972 OUP NY

Woll A. "Black Musical Theatre from Coontown to Dream Girls"1989 Louisiana State University Press Baton Rouge

Wood B. "The Song For Me" E book CD version 24 November 2003

Appendix 1

<u>Jelly Roll Morton's demonstration of *La Praline Quadrille* ex Library of Congress interview with Alan Lomax.</u>[205]

(Rounder CD 1091 contains Morton's words and the musical examples.) Morton's words are in bold face:

"And this ... *Tiger Rag* happened to be transformed from an old Quadrille that was in many different tempos. And I'll no doubt give you an idea how it went. This was the introduction, meaning that everyone was supposed to get their partner

Plays Tiger Rag introduction

Get your partners. Everybody get your partners. People would be rushing around the hall getting their partners. And maybe ... have maybe five minutes lapsed between that time. And of course they'd start it over again. And that was the first part.

Plays Tiger Rag introduction (repeated)

And the next strain would be a waltz strain, I believe.

Plays Tiger Rag waltz strain

That would be the waltz strain.

---

205 Transcription from Mike Meddings website www.doctorjazz.co.uk

Also they'd have another strain that comes right belong ... right beside it.

Tiger Rag third strain (begun)

It's a mazooka time.

Tiger Rag third strain (concluded)

Of course that was that ... third strain. And of course they had another strain. And ... that was in a different tempo.

Tiger Rag fourth strain (begun)

Interviewer: What kind of time is that?

That's a two-four time.

Tiger Rag fourth strain (concluded)

Of course they had another one.

Interviewer: That makes five.

Yeah.

Tiger Rag fifth strain

Now I will show you how it was transformed. It happened to be transformed by your performer at this ... particular time. *Tiger Rag* for your approval.

Interviewer: Who named it the Tiger Rag?

I also named it. Came from the way that I played it by making the ... tiger on my elbow. And I also named it.

A person said once, "It sounds like a tiger hollerin'."

**I said, "Fine."
To myself, I said "That's the name."**

So I'll play it for you.

Tiger Rag transformation (begun)

Tiger Rag transformation (continued)

Hold that tiger.

Tiger Rag transformation (concluded)

That was many years before the Dixieland had ever started, when I played the *Tiger Rag*."

Note: The name of the Quadrille has always been speculative. Jack Stewart said Morton called it *'La Marseillaise'*.[206] Others called it *La Praline*. Stewart said that the name *Praline* was used for the trio of what was later called *Sensation Rag*.[207] Jack Laine mentioned *Praline* as a number written by Achille (Baquet)[208]. Later, a tune called *Praline* was recorded by Tony Parenti but this was a moody Creole blues.[209] I have decided to use the name *La Praline* mainly to avoid confusion with the French national anthem.

---

206 Stewart J. in Jazz Archivist Vol XV p26/7
207 Stewart J. The Jazz Archivist Vol XV p27
208 Cover note by Edmond Souchon on a World Record Club recording called Papa Laine's Children.
209 Circle 78 inch record CO 105

Appendix 2

A Guide to the Performance of Early Jazz

(This guide has been adapted from the guide prepared by the author in 2004 to brief members of the Buddy Bolden Orchestra prior to the first rehearsal.)

Contents

Introduction

Section 1 Ensemble Performance Practice
1. Instrumentation
2. Ensemble Improvisation

Section 2 The Front Line
1. Notes for the Violinist
2. Cornet Improvisation
4. The Clarinet Style
5. Playing Valve Trombone

Section 3 Rhythm
1. Bass
2. Guitar
3. Drums
4. Dance Rhythms

Section 4 Repertoire and Vocal Performance
List of Bolden Band Tunes

Introduction

This guide is based on the research of the Author previously published in *"The Loudest Trumpet: Buddy Bolden and the Early History of Jazz"* and *"Exploring Early Jazz: The Origins and Evolution of the New Orleans Style"*.

Information from oral history resources and published accounts indicates that the early jazz dance music played between 1896 and 1908 differed to some extent from that of musicians who were recorded after 1917 when the first jazz recordings became available. Instrumentation and performance practices from that early era (known as the Elemental Jazz period) have been established from the above written sources and from performances by early musicians, whose recordings, made in the 1940's and later, demonstrate vestiges of the earlier style. In the latter respect the jazz historian is more fortunate than specialists recreating classical early music styles who have had to rely solely on documentary sources.

> "After 1900 the Bolden style was progressively adopted to varying degrees by other dance bands. Most of the bands retained a four instrument front line: violin leader, cornet, valve trombone and clarinet sometimes pitched in C major. During this time some black players continued to play traditional music from published scores. After 1900 significant information also becomes available that indicates a stream of white bands playing both improvised and arranged syncopated. music. At the end of its first decade, however, the blues based jazz style introduced by Buddy Bolden remained essentially unchanged. Donald Marquis called this music basic or **Elemental Jazz**.
>
> In its second decade, between 1907 and 1917 Elemental Jazz became enmeshed in experimentation with outside influences; traditional march music, tango, Tin Pan Alley rags and march one steps, Classical Ragtime, and composed blues. Some bands introduced these styles through written scores, though others tried to play them by developing their own informal memorised routines—a kind of **Free Ragtime**. White bands were increasingly active in this decade, participating in the development

of the new music. During this period the slide trombone became the instrument of choice, enabling the development of the tailgate style of trombone playing, and the consequent multi voiced polyphony that characterised New Orleans jazz. The four beat Memphis beat was introduced.

By about 1915 the style had been crystallised, with the transmutation of rags marches and blues, through free ragtime, into a style of New Orleans jazz that was later to become known as **Classic Jazz**.

In 1917 at the beginning of the third decade of Early Jazz, a white band made the first jazz recording, and the Jazz Age commenced. Because of the new international recording industry jazz soon became a worldwide fashion. The first part of the decade 1917/27 also saw the refinement of the **Classic Jazz** style culminating in the style of the King Oliver Creole Jazz Band playing in Chicago. Sophisticated head arrangements were introduced along with complex three-part counter point. Prearranged breaks and set piece solos were introduced. Then the saxophone gradually became part of the New Orleans ensemble.

After 1924 very few small New Orleans style groups played except in recording studios. Big Bands became fashionable by that time, largely dominating the dance band market. During this **Studio Jazz** phase more formal arrangements were introduced to ensemble passages, and by 1927 full chorus improvised solos were being played by all the bands large and small.

Four Phases of Early Jazz in Summary:

1. **1897/1907 Elemental Jazz** Buddy Bolden ragged freely improvised dance songs and blues
2. **1907/17 Free Ragtime** Classical Rag and March forms were adapted to the New Orleans style.

3. **1917/23 Classic Jazz** Ensemble style head arrangements were refined and perfected.

4. **1924/27 Studio Jazz** The soloist emerged along with nascent ensemble arrangements."[210]

The guide is intended to assist jazz musicians wishing to perform authentic New Orleans Jazz music of the period 1896 to 1908 but indications will also be given to assist interpretations of music from the transition period 1907/1917 during which changes were occurring that led to the Classic Jazz of 1917-1927.

Section 1
Ensemble Performance Practice

1. Instrumentation

The improvising dance bands that began performing jazz music in New Orleans after 1896 were in many respects similar in organization to the conventional dance bands they began to replace. Almost all relied on a violinist leader, and the normal composition was violin, cornet, clarinet, valve trombone, guitar, bass violin and trap drums. There were some early experiments with other instrumentations; Buddy Bolden's band utilised two clarinets in the front line on some occasions though the violin was also commonly employed in that band. The Eagle Band used a piccolo lead on some occasions though that band too settled into a traditional pattern with a violinist leader.

(a) **Violins**

Steel violin strings were not used until well into the 20th Century, so the use of gut strings would appear to have been normal except for the G string. During the 19th Century the normal stringing was gut on the three upper strings and overspun close wound (silver) G string. Because of the recent emphasis on authentic instrumentation for the performance of Baroque Music, the above strings are once more available and are recommended for authentic performance of Elemental Jazz.

---

[210] Excerpts from Exploring Early Jazz by Daniel Hardie 2002

(b) Piccolo

The Eagle Band that was the descendant of Bolden's Orchestra apparently sometimes used a piccolo leader (Bab Frank) and this player was also leader of some other orchestras. Photographs show him using a wooden flute and piccolo with ivory mouthpieces.

(c) The Cornet

Short model cornets pitched in Bb were used by all bands. This type of instrument is still widely used in brass bands and should be readily available. It would be an advantage to have a shank tuning to A natural for use in sharp keys.

The later long model cornet which has a different tone quality should not be used for authentic performance of early jazz. Trumpets were never used.

Cup mutes appear to have been used by some players and some witnesses suggested that Buddy Bolden used such a tin cup mute.

(d) Clarinets

Albert system clarinets pitched in Bb and C major were used in most early jazz orchestras and some players appear also to have had instruments pitched in A major. Some players used metal clarinets. Clarinets pitched in Eb were used in street bands. Boehm system clarinets did not appear in jazz until the 1920's and should not be used to perform authentic early jazz.

Though some authorities suggest that Bolden's band used a C clarinet melody lead with an improvising Bb second, the only photograph of the band shows two Bb instruments.

(e) Valve Trombone

Most early jazz bands employed short model tenor valve trombones pitched in Bb of the type then common in brass bands. By 1910 however some bands were employing slide trombones. In general, for early jazz before 1908 it is better to use the valve instrument that is not capable of the type of tailgate performance style that only came into vogue around 1913.

Because of its construction the tone of the valve trombone also differs significantly from that of the valve trombone.

A "constant need to correct intonation by embouchure", and "stuffiness resulting from tight bends in the wind way" are described as leading to its characteristic sound. It is however more flexible in some rapid passagework.

(f) **Bass Violin**

Some of the early musicians used three stringed basses but the majority had a four stringed instrument. As with the violin steel strings were not available. The instrument was always bowed, or only very occasionally plucked, so a bow is needed for authentic early jazz performance.

(g) **Guitar**

The six stringed Spanish guitar appears in all major bands of the early jazz period. Bolden's guitarist used a large bodied guitar identified as similar to the Martin Flat Top a type introduced as early as 1857 and still being manufactured. Early photographs show that this type of guitar was universally employed in the early jazz era. These guitars were not supplied with metal strings until 1922. A flat top guitar should be used for authentic performance. Moulded and metal top guitars are a later innovation. Gut guitar strings are also preferred for authentic performance. Nylon strings were not introduced until the 1940's.

(h) **Trap Drums**

The first trap drum set appeared around 1896 and was quickly adopted by the jazz bands. It consisted of a large, brass band type; rope braced bass drum with a homemade foot pedal and one snare drum. Most drummers had one (12"/15") cymbal attached to the bass drum, though some photos do not show a cymbal. For authentic performance dampers should not be used on the bass drum, which should be allowed to ring like a marching bass drum. Small bass drums should not be used.

Marching type wood-rimmed snare drums were used, originally tied to the bass drum or leaning against a chair, but more commonly on their own stands. Both drums should have pigskin, not synthetic, heads.

Wood blocks and other traps did not appear until after 1910. Swats or brushes were not used at that time.

2. Ensemble Improvisation

The early improvising bands were performing a transitional type of music, taking the regular dance music of the New Orleans dance halls, and converting it to what was later to be known as jazz.

They were said to play mainly in Bb, but sometimes in F and Eb.

Tempo was not as fast as that of jazz bands after 1917, and rhythm was suited to the dance steps of the time, two step march tempo, three four waltzes and Quadrille movements including mazurka, polka, and the slower slow drag, and schottisches.

Most were known as Chorus bands, that is, they didn't play the verses and codas of popular songs, only the choruses, but sometimes composed their own endings. This included Buddy Bolden's band and it's successor Frank Duson's Eagle Band

Their regular practice was to emphasise the melody which was carried at all times, usually by the violinist leader.

The violinist beat in the time and led the performance as was normal in the traditional dance orchestra setting. One witness said that in the first chorus they all played the melody straight.

Thereafter the individual members improvised paraphrases on the melody, ragging the tune by varying the duration and emphasis of individual cadences in an informal raggy manner, called by some musicologists heterophony (This was to become a looser Free Ragtime in the next decade.)

There were no whole chorus solos; so, to provide variety the melody line was passed around, with one instrument restating the melody in the foreground while others ragged behind the lead. (The violin continued to state the melody.)

Breaks and trombone bass runs were also introduced to provide variety, as had been done in the earlier brass band compositions.

Variety was further provided by variation in volume. Bolden's band played very loudly but on some choruses the volume was dropped to allow the rhythm to come through. This created an elementary swing. (Bolden is said to have said to play it sweet and low so he could hear the swish of the dancer's feet.)

In the blues the Spanish habanera beat was sometimes introduced in such choruses.

The bands also sang extempore vocal choruses to add variety. The best known of these was Bolden's *Funky Butt*.

Last chorus they "All bust out loud".

Most bands consisted of a mixture of readers and ear players or fakers. In order to meet the above requirements the violinist leader needed to know all the tunes or have a stock of lead sheets. It is said that clarinettist Frank Lewis carried around a set of such stock lead sheets for the Bolden Band.

Bands learned the melody from the lead sheets or by listening to others, and worked out their own head arrangements.

Section 2
The Front Line

1. Notes for the Violinist

You are responsible for the establishment of tempo and maintaining the cohesion of the performance by maintaining focus on the melody.

There are few indications about violin playing style in the oral history, though many witnesses said how important the role of the violinist was in providing the melodic support for the improvising players.

Fortunately we have recordings by two of the "best violinists" in New Orleans. Peter Bocage (Original Superior Orchestra) and Armand Piron (Eagle Band, Peerless Orchestra and King Oliver's first band). Piron who later led his own Orchestra was regarded as the best of the New Orleans violinists.

The appropriate style is simple rather dry melody with little or no vibrato. You are not a folk fiddler or a concert performer. There are none of the violin gymnastics performed by later jazz violinists like Stephan Grappelli.

In some choruses the melody will need to be played above the stave in order to be heard. There you will sometimes encounter the clarinet. Leave him to twiddle. Concentrate on melody. Sometimes the melody should be played quietly in the lower register behind another player who has taken over the melodic statement.

Simple glissandi, slides and simple ornaments should be added to achieve effects. A touch of melancholy appears in some violin melodic statements particularly in the blues. One early violinist was said to have played everything in double stops.

As a guide, listen to Peter Bocage playing with the Love-Jiles Orchestra Riverside CD OJCCD-1835-2 and especially Armand Piron with his own orchestra on Azure AZ-CD-13 on which various performances of *West Indies Blues* and *Mama's Gone Goodbye* are illustrative of the correct style. The Louis James String Band CD (American Music AMCD-14) includes a melody line for *Funky Butt*, schottisches and other relevant early violin tunes. The recordings of the New Orleans Ragtime Orchestra are also instructive. (*Creole Belles, Winin' Boy Blues* and *St. Louis Tickle* on Yazoo CD420)

2. Cornet Improvisation

While most of the early bands had violinist leaders they were all associated with star cornetists, Buddy Bolden, Freddy Keppard and the young Bunk Johnson for example, and King Oliver came into the Eagle Band around 1910.

You are free to improvise except on first choruses and even there you can play slight variations on the melody.

Bolden was a loud player, as was Keppard. Bolden was also able to play soft and low and sweetly. Bunk "followed Buddy with his sweetness but could never play rough and hard like Bolden". Keppard could. In the blues Bolden put in moans and groans like a Baptist preacher. Keppard took the instrument up into the high register. Some said Keppard was the player who most played like Bolden. Others said Wooden Joe Nicholas sounded like him.

Humphrey Lyttleton described Keppard's playing as based on an eight to the bar ragtime foundation. That is to say lots of double quavers (half beats) and four quaver staccato runs. He drew attention to a fast shimmering vibrato Keppard shared with his contemporaries. Keppard also used blue notes, slurs, smears and blurred triple tongued ornaments. He used runs on the open tones (they called them the bugle notes.)

Punch Miller said, "Keppard played sweet when sober but got rough when drunk."

In slower blues Bunk Johnson's style (without blunders) is appropriate. When he was young he was said to have a tone and attack like Bobby Hackett. Many of the staccato improvisational techniques appropriate for the period are illustrated in Bunk's demonstrations of

Bolden's style. Bolden apparently had a pet phrase he put in everywhere he could fit it.[211]

All of the above are available to you in playing authentic early jazz. Keppard's style with a touch of Wooden Joe's tone would seem ideal.

You should listen to Keppard playing *Stockyard Strut, Adam's Apple, Messin Around* and *Salty Dog*. (HotnSweet Records New Orleans Giants Vol 2 #15222). Wooden Joe on American Music AMCD 5 and Bunk Johnson's demonstration of the Bolden Style *Bolden Medley* on American Music CD AMCD 16. Bunk Johnson playing *All the Girls Go Crazy, Careless Love and 2/19 Blues* (Goodtime Jazz LP)

4. The Clarinet Style

Three major clarinettists who participated in the transition to jazz made enough recordings between them to permit some conclusions to be made about the Early Jazz style. They were Alphonse Picou, Louis Big Eye Nelson and George Baquet. George Baquet's brother Achille Baquet also recorded (with white bands) in a similar style.

None of those players used significant vibrato. (That probably appeared with Bechet and Dodds after 1912).

This early style concentrated to a considerable extent on melody and harmony with some excursions into the upper register. Improvisations made considerable use of ascending and descending quaver arpeggios. When the clarinet was brought into the foreground for a chorus the players often began with a few bars of straight melody before embarking on their improvisations. Though solos are not played in early jazz this pattern would apply in choruses where the clarinet is brought forward to carry the theme.

Clarinet improvisations appear to have had the same eight to the bar foundation as cornet arpeggios but used alternately slurred and articulated pairs of notes in their ascending and descending runs in relation to the underlying melody.[212]

Picou said his approach to ragging was to introduce eight or sixteen notes to the bar, and he used arpeggios or runs to do this, creating cross rhythms by alternating the use of slurs and accented notes. This also created a kind of simple counter point.

---

211 See Hardie Daniel "The Loudest Trumpet" 2000 p40
212 see Exploring Early Jazz by Daniel Hardie p245

Importantly for the sound of early jazz, the earliest Creole players appear to have been trained in the French school of playing. Theogene Baquet and Lorenzo Tio who taught many of the younger players were skilled exponents. More importantly the Creole players spoke French patois, and this is apparent in the intonation of French speaking players. It influences the tonal qualities of their playing, as the player's characteristic vowel sounds are used in forming notes on the clarinet and so modify the tone produced. The French school also employed a mouthpiece with a characteristically narrow lay and a soft reed that encouraged fluency at the expense of volume of sound. Players like Alphonse Picou were not loud players like many players of the 1920's.

Big Eye Louis Nelson was critical of Picou's playing saying it was soulless; he said you had to put in some whining everywhere you can consistent with the melody. Nevertheless, he too, used a lot of arpeggio playing.

Good examples of this style are to be heard on American Music CD 44 (both Picou and Nelson) and Nelson alone on AMCD 7. George Baquet recorded with Jelly Roll Morton on Classics CD-627CD.

5. Playing Valve Trombone

Because of its nature the valve trombone prevented the use of glissandi and accordingly tailgate trombone did not appear in the early jazz era. (Jack Carey and Kid Ory forged the style in around 1913.)

Many of the early valve trombonists were brass band performers and it appears they adapted brass band trombone to Early Jazz. This style appears to have been based on bass vamping along with bass runs of the type used in brass band marches. In Bolden's band Will Cornish apparently pioneered the use of valve trombone breaks.

Early trombonist Roy Palmer said that vamping was the foundation of the trombone role, and that the trombonist should only depart from it for short periods. It seems that the trombonist could also on occasions play melody. Bebe Ridgley said that it was fundamentally a bass part but sometimes filled in open spots, played harmony with another horn or played the melody.

Unfortunately because the valve trombone went out of use there are no recordings of the style. However a witness said that Albert Warner, playing slide trombone in a ragtime performance, sounded like Buddy Bolden's valve trombonist Frank Duson. On that occasion Warner appears to be playing from a score and has some trouble with phrases that would have been simple on a valve instrument. While some commentators said that Warner's style was too brass band influenced and unsuitable for the jazz bands of the 1940's in which he played, it seems it would have been better suited to the earlier valve trombone style. He was considered to be "one of the last and most exciting exponents of an earlier tradition in which the trombone combined its function of sustaining the rhythmic foundation with that of providing the bass voice."

Players like Roy Palmer and Zue Robertson appear to have carried much of their vamping style over to early recordings using a slide instrument.

Albert Warner can be heard on Riverside CD OJCCD-1835-2 and Zue Robertson plays a solid vamp style in Jelly Roll Morton's *London Blues* (Masters of Jazz MJCD 19).

Section 3
Rhythm

Rhythm is at the heart of the transition from late 19th century dance music to improvised jazz. This occurred at the same time as Ragtime became popular and it is apparent that the same raggy vernacular music, jigs, reels and jump ups played a part in the birth of both forms of music. In Bolden's band the influence of the rhythms of the spiritual singers in the Uptown Baptist churches was the foundation for the type of rhythm he played.

It was two beat. That is to say that it emphasised the first and third beats of the four beat bar. Apparently he and other Uptown Musicians even adapted the rhythms of waltzes and Quadrilles to their extroverted type of performance with added emphasis within the traditional rhythms to induce a swing.

1. Bass Violin

The foundation for the two beat rhythm is what is called an oompah bass. The bass plays on beats one and three. This was usually played arco though on some occasions a bass was plucked for emphasis. One early bass player said that the bowed bass sometimes improvised counter melodies in the blues.

2. Guitar

The Spanish guitar seems to have come into the first jazz bands via street music. Many Spanish musicians played in the streets of New Orleans at that time.

Buddy Bolden's guitarist is said to have introduced the technique of hitting through all notes of the chord. (Bud Scott claimed to have invented the technique of playing "four beats straight down")

The guitar played all four beats in duple time emphasising the second and fourth beats. The emphasis on the after beats appears to be necessary to mimic the offbeat clapping of the congregations in the Holy Roller churches. Some players introduced shuffle beats or double beats on the second and fourth beats.

John St Cyr said that the guitarists played all four beats with emphasis on beats two and four and sometimes added little runs for emphasis.

George Guesnon said that early players played "rolling chords":C to G7; C to C7; F back to C; C back to G but did not play minor, augmented or diminished chords.[213]

3. Trap Drums

The Trap drum kit was a new invention (ca 1896). Dee Dee Chandler who sometimes played with Bolden had improvised a rather clumsy set of levers attached to a wooden foot pedal and hinged to the top rim of a large rope braced brass band bass drum. He formerly played snare drum in John Robichaux's Orchestra (Robichaux played the bass drum). Chandler then also tied his snare drum to the rim of the bass drum, enabling him to play both drums. Robichaux was then able to move to 1st violin.

Brass band bass drums of the time had a cymbal mounted centrally on the top, (played by the bass drummer with his bass drum stick) but, because of his cumbersome lever foot pedal arrangement, Chandler had to mount his (approx 15") cymbal vertically on the rim at the right hand side of the drum facing him. This meant he could play the cymbal with his snare drum sticks. Other early drummers quickly copied his kit and even as late as 1917 his lever system was still in use. However most drummers soon had the snare drum on it's own stand. The cymbal was usually mounted on the top of the bass drum in a variety of ways.

---

[213] Russel New Orleans Style p77

The early drummers were not all badly trained but had been taught traditional techniques like the press roll (drag), paradiddle and flam or flim flam. The press roll was a prized formula. One player apparently used a continuous press roll called 'the steady roll' that accented the second and fourth beats while remaining steady.

Early Jazz drumming followed the same two beat formula mentioned above. The bass drum only beat on 1 and 3. The snare drum either beat only 2 and 4 or beat all four with emphasis placed on 2 and 4 as recommended for guitar. One early musician recommended the bass drum play 1 and 3 with a press roll on snare on 2 and 4 as the ideal pattern. Brass band bass drummers apparently played the cymbal primarily on the after beats.

A good example of the two-beat drumming style can be heard on the 1927 recording *Come On and Stomp Stomp Stomp* by Johnny Dodds Black Bottom Stompers.

4. Dance Rhythms

When playing traditional dances like the waltz, schottische, and Quadrille movements the drummer and other rhythm instrumentalists needed to adapt to the needs of the dancers as summarised in the following excerpts from *The Loudest Trumpet: Buddy Bolden and the Early History of Jazz:*

"The time signature used would be determined by the item being played and especially the dance to be performed. One Steps and Two Steps had their own rhythmic logic, as did Waltzes and Schottisches. These old dances were not played in a simple rhythm but had rhythmic stresses—emphases that were necessary for correct performance of the dance and in popular practice these were probably somewhat overemphasised to accentuate the swings and turns of the dance.

Baby Dodds said of the mazurka …"(it is) *in three four time. But there is one little catch to this three four. Always at the end of every measure its got a little accented 'boomp boomp'—two eighth notes. and then you pick up three four time again.* "[214] It has also been suggested that the waltz, properly performed is the rhythm of a swing and the polka as having a "a very energetic jump".[215]

---

214 Russel W New Orleans Style 1994 p 44
215 Quirey Brenda May I Have The Pleasure 1976/87 p 68

John St Cyr said these dances were usually performed at an easy tempo so as not to tire the dancers. He described the Schottische as a very beautiful dance that needed a slow tempo quoting the tempos of *"Sophisticated Lady"* and *"The Stars fell on Alabama"* as perfect for the Schottische.[216] The underlying rhythms of the Schottische can also be heard on a recording of *"Sweet Adeline"* (1903) played as a Schottische by the Louis James String Band.[217] On this same CD there is a very good demonstration of how a waltz (*"After the Ball"*) would have been played in practice at a local dance, and a Quadrille fragment played in a March rhythm not unlike the way the old time Barn Dance used to be performed. The same group played *"Funky Butt"* in a very laid back 4/4.

The Rhythms of the Dance Steps

Each of the dances mentioned by witnesses as part of the Bolden repertoire has its own rhythm expressed by dance teachers as stresses within the four beat bar (measure). The best-known example of these is the **Waltz**, where commonly the stress is placed on the first beat of the 3/4 measure by slightly elongating it. so {—...}.

The **Quadrille** did not have a set pattern but borrowed patterns from other dances, like the mazurka; a typical Quadrille in early New Orleans would possibly have included waltz, mazurka and polka rhythms.

The **Mazurka** has been described as having an even (3/4) rhythm with an accent on the second beat, thus {...—...} but the last step of the three to a measure is a little hop.

The **Schottische** is in 4/4 time but consists of three running steps and a hop to the measure the rhythm being described as even with a stress on the first beat of the measure, as {—...}.

The **Two Step** rhythm is uneven (2/4 or less commonly 4/4) with three steps to a measure and a stress on the first step—in 2/4 {...and...}.

---

216 Russel W.op cit 1994 p 271/272
217 American Music CD AMCD-14

The **Polka** also in 2/4 has a peculiar uneven rhythm with four steps to the measure with a stress on a hop that occurs on the pick up beat. {—and ... hup}

The **One Step** is a quick walking step with one step to every beat. {...} or {...}—a ragtime dance.

The **Foxtrot** derived from the One Step and the Two Step was originally in 2/4 but later a smoother 4/4. It combines quick and slow steps. A faster version is the Quickstep. In 4/4 steps are taken one measure quick {...} then 1 measure slow {—}. This dance is sometimes performed in cut common time. (¢). As it arrived around 1914, it is unlikely Bolden would have heard of it but it became the basis of Classical Jazz performances in the 1920's usually in 4/4 time.[218]

In practice a certain amount of experimentation will be required to establish the correct rhythmic formula for each of the dances to be performed especially when emulating the boisterous Uptown adaptation of these dances.

Section 4
Repertoire and Vocal Performance

While it is certain that the bands of the Bolden Era sang vocal interpretations of the lyrics of the songs they performed little is known about the vocal interpretation. They did adapt the words to suit the occasion. *Funky Butt*, which was an old river folk song, is a good example. Another is their adaptation of the lyrics of the traditional folk song *The Old Cow Died*. Played to the first theme of *Muskrat Ramble* this became *Old Brock Cried When The Old Cow Died* with jibes aimed at the guitar player Brock Mumford. The folk reel *Run Nigger Run* in the hands of the Bolden band became *Run Strumpet Run*. Some may have been sung by individual band members others by the full band. Examples of similar singing style might be *Any Rags* as sung by Johnny St Cyr on AMCD-5 or *Everybody's Talkin About Sammy* and *Down By the Riverside* (Sam Morgan's Band on Jazz Oracle CD BDW8002)

---

218 Hardie Daniel *"The Loudest Trumpet"* 2000 pp 88/89

There are some partial lyrics attributed to the Bolden band and others from sources such as Jelly Roll Morton's Library of Congress recordings.

List of Bolden Band Tunes

Research by Ingemar Wågerman and Froggy May has produced a list of some 60 songs possibly played by the Bolden band and they have identified recorded performances of many of them. Many of these attributions are speculative but the attached list appears to be a conservative one. Lyrics, lead sheets and even midi files are available for most of them. One or two have not been located either as score or recorded performance though oral evidence suggests that they did form part of the repertoire.

Those marked (A) in the list below were almost certainly in the repertoire. Though those marked (B) are less certain it is likely they were included. Other bands like the Eagle band are also known to have played a similar repertoire.

<u>Sub group A—tunes almost certainly in the repertoire</u>

(A) ALL THE GIRLS (Whores) GO CRAZY ABOUT THE WAY I WALK (Ride)

(A) ANY RAGS?

(A) BOWERY BUCK (a Tom Turpin Rag)

(A) BUCKET'S GOT A HOLE IN IT

(A) CARELESS LOVE Traditional
Many old New Orleans bands preceded the Careless Love tune with a 12 bar blues

(A) DON'T GO WAY NOBODY

(A) FROG LEGS RAG (James Scott Rag)

(A) FUNKY BUTT, (Aka—"I Thought I Heard Buddy Bolden Say"; "Mr Bolden's Song"; "Buddy Bolden's Blues"; "Doin the Ping Pong")

(A) GET OUT OF HERE

(A) GO DOWN MOSES (Spiritual)

(A) HOME SWEET HOME

(A) IDA SWEET AS APPLE CIDER

(A) IF YOU DON'T SHAKE, YOU DON'T GET NO CAKE aka—Mama's Got A Baby or TI-NA-NA, "Mama's Got a Baby Named Tee-Na-Na". Includes "I May Be Crazy But I Ain't No Fool"

(A) MAKE ME A PALLET ON THE FLOOR

(A) MAKIN' RUNS

(A) MAPLE LEAF RAG (Scott Joplin) Note some authorities said Bolden did not play these rags)

(A) MR JOHNSON, TURN ME LOOSE

(A) PALM LEAF RAG Slow drag (Scott Joplin)

(A) RIDE ON KING (Jesus) (Spiritual) (Possible alternative title "Ride On Conquering King ")

(A) SALTY DOG

(A) THE OLD COW DIED ("The Old Cow Died and Old Brock Cried") (Muskrat Ramble strain 1 according to Sydney Bechet)

(A) TIGER RAG (Quadrille) aka LA PRALINE

(A) TWO-NINETEEN TOOK MY BABY AWAY (aka TWO-NINETEEN BLUES, MAMIE'S BLUES)

(B) Tunes mentioned by witnesses of which less is known or the attribution is less certain * indicates a tune that was probably in the repertoire

(B) DON'T SEND ME NO ROSES 'CAUSE SHOES IS WHAT I NEED (not found)

(B) GETTYSBURG MARCH (Some doubt here as published too late in 1911or12—may have been folk march earlier—(the title suggests a Civil War origin).

(B) GET YOUR BIG LEGS OFF OF ME*

(B) IDAHO—A WILD WESTERN FANTASIA*

(B) IF THE MAN IN THE MOON WERE A COON*

(B) I'M GOING WHEN JESUS CALLS ME (not found)

(B) INDIAN SAGWA (Published ca1915)

(B) IF YOU DON'T LIKE MY POTATOES WHY DO YOU DIG SO DEEP*
(Also a blues)

(B) JOYCE 76 (As yet unknown)

(B) LAZY MOON*

(B) LET ME BE YOUR LI'L DOG TILL YOUR BIG DOG COMES (Blues?)

(B) MELPOMENE STREET BLUES (possibly Melpomene Mazurka by G Williams)

(B) MOONWINKS (Mazurka)*

(B) EMANCIPATION DAY*

(B) PANAMA RAG (Seymour)*

(B) PRETTY, PRETTY MAMA, OPEN YOUR LEGS ONE MORE TIME (not found)

(B) RUN STRUMPET RUN*
(Possibly a Bolden profane version of *Run Nigger Run*)

(B) SAMMY SAMSON (May be *Makin Runs* or *Happy Sammy* F.C Schmitt 1906)

(B) SHOO, SKEETER SHOO*

(B) STICK IT WHERE YOU STUCK IT LAST NIGHT (not found)

(B) THE HOUSE GOT READY (nothing known yet)

(B) WAIT TIL' THE SUN SHINES NELLIE*

About the Author

Daniel Hardie is a jazz historian and former clarinetist. He is also a maritime artist and historian and has published a number of maritime historical works and exhibited his Sea Heritage paintings in Australian cities and in Sydney where he lives. He is married and has two grown daughters.

Hardie is also the author of three previous works on early jazz history—*The Loudest Trumpet: Buddy Bolden and the Early History of Jazz*, 2000; *Exploring Early Jazz: The Origins and Evolution of the New Orleans Style*, 2002; and *The Ancestry of Jazz: A Musical Family History* published by iUniverse in 2004.

Index

Musical compositions are shown in *italics*

Abbie Brunies' Band, 1
ad-lib performance, 31
African shout music, 4
Afro-American accent, 90
Afro-American music, 73, 103
Afro American vernacular dances, 23
Albert (simple) system clarinets, 77
Albert System, 23
Alexander Adolph, 113
Allemandes, 2
Allen Brass Band, 115
All the Whores Like the Way I Ride, 52, 53
Amsterdam Dance House, 22
Anniversary Song, 20
Any Rags, 41, 90
Archaeological analogy, 76, 96
Archaeologists, 96
Archaeologists model, 130
Archaeology, 121, 122
Architectural sketch or model, 96
Artesian Hall, 12
Artisan (Artesian) Hall, 13
Asbury Herbert, 22, 133

Ascona jazz festival, 81
Augustat Boo Boo, 107, 108

balance of sound, 85
Balle, 11
ballrooms, 2
balls, 2, 17
bands of music, 3, 23
bands of the first generation, 79
bandstands, 8, 13
Baptist, 4, 13, 17, 25, 30, 61, 64, 70, 151, 154
Baptist preacher, 64
Baquet, Achille 141, 152
Baquet George, 17, 18, 59, 117, 141, 152, 153
Bailey Buster, 75
barbershops, 26
Barker Danny, 18, 58, 70, 102
Barnyard Blues, 111
barrelhouse, 52
barrelhouses, 4, 22
bass violin, 4, 24, 27, 31, 32, 68, 77, 87, 88, 115, 146

Bates John, 77, 79, 82, 85
Bechet Sydney, 49, 54, 57, 104, 152, 160
beer halls, 22, 34, 51
Bigeou Esther, 129
Bill Gallaty's High Rollers, 116
Birth of Jazz, 1
birth of jazz, xv, 1, 5, 7, 9, 24
Bishop Sir Henry, 44
Black origins, 7
Blind Boone, 59
Blind Boone's Rag Medley, 74
Bloxsome Ian, 78, 81
Blue Ribbon Social Club, 17
blues, xiv, 8, 12, 16, 18, 21, 22, 25, 30, 31, 33, 35, 38, 39, 40, 44, 51, 54, 55, 57, 58, 59, 60, 61, 68, 70, 72, 74, 81, 86, 88, 91, 93, 94, 98, 99, 101, 103, 105, 123, 124, 125, 127, 141, 144, 145, 150, 151, 154, 159, 161
boatmen, 55
Bocage Peter, 68, 99, 112, 115, 125, 126
Boiusseaux H.J., 58
Bolden Charles Buddy, xiii, xiv, xv, 7, 8, 9, 10, 12, 13,14, 15, 16, 17, 18, 19, 20, 22, 24, 25,27, 29, 30, 31, 33, 34, 36, 37, 38, 39,40, 42, 43, 44, 45, 46, 47, 48, 49, 51,52, 53, 54, 55, 56, 57, 58, 59, 60, 61, 62, 63, 64, 66, 67, 68, 69, 70, 71, 72, 73, 74, 76, 77, 78, 80, 81, 82, 87, 89, 90, 91, 92, 93, 94, 95, 97, 98, 99, 101, 102, 103, 104, 105, 107, 109, 110, 111, 112, 113, 114, 117, 118, 120, 122, 123, 124, 125, 126, 127, 128, 130, 131, 135, 136, 143, 144, 145, 146, 147, 148, 149, 150, 151, 152, 153, 154, 155, 156, 157, 158, 159, 160, 162
Bolden's band, 30, 113
Bolden Cylinder recording, 73
Bolden Era, 92, 117, 118, 127, 128, 129, 130
Boul Boul's string band, 108
bowed bass, 84, 88, 113, 124, 154
Bowery Buck, 48
Boyce Retaw, 78, 81
Brass bands, 3
brass bands, 4, 23, 24, 118, 147
brass instruments, 4, 24, 69, 86, 87, 115
breakdown dances, 23
Breaks, 72, 149
breaks, 54, 64, 71, 73, 74, 85, 88, 91, 104, 105, 145, 153
broken rhythms, 119
Broun Heywood Hale, 121
Brown Tom, 6, 116
Buchanan John, 81, 83
buck and wing figures', 48
Buddy Bolden's Birthday, 81
Buddy Bolden Revival Orchestra, 36, 82, 92, 103
Bull Geoff, 77, 81, 82
Bush Dance Club of Bendigo, 46

cabarets, 8, 22, 115
Cable Mary, xiii, 107, 133
Cakewalk, 55
Cakewalk in the Sky, 55
Cakewalks, 15, 43, 91, 136
cakewalks, 93, 119

California, 108, 113, 117, 128, 133, 134, 135
can can, 22
Canal St, 2
Careless Love, 57, 58, 83, 152, 159
Caribbean music, 102
Carey Jack, 45, 94, 105, 115, 116, 123, 153
C clarinet, 90
cellos, 3, 23
Celtic origin, 47
Charles Galloway's band, 8
Charters Sam, xiv, 8, 12, 28, 30, 32, 45, 52
Cheapskate Hall, 12
chorus band, 125
Chorus bands, 72, 149
church music, 31
Civil War, 3, 4, 8, 12, 23, 43, 55, 63, 134, 161
clarinet, 4, 23, 24, 26, 29, 68, 69, 71, 77, 85, 86, 87, 89, 90, 92, 93, 94, 104, 115, 124, 125, 126, 130, 144, 146, 147, 150, 152, 153
Classical Piano Rags, 48
classical rags, 34, 67
Classic Jazz, 7, 111, 119, 123, 145, 146
Classic Jazz Era, 111
classical music, 9
Classic Rags, 111
Classic rags, 94, 102
classic rags, 94
Clem Brothers Orchestra, 109
clodoche, 22
Colonial Period, 2

Collins Richard, 11, 30, 100, 110
Collins Wallace, 33, 68
Come On and Stomp Stomp Stomp, 92
computer simulations, 96
concert-saloons, 4, 22
concert performances, 36, 95, 98
concerts, 4, 78, 84
Contemporary Repertoire, 78
Continentals, 14
Contrabands, 62
conventional dances, 33, 38
Conventional Dance Tunes, 45
coon, 39, 64
coonjine, 40
Coonjine Song, 40
Coon Novelty, 39
Coon Song, 39, 40, 41, 42, 43, 86, 90, 91, 99, 113
Coon Songs, 39, 42, 44, 45, 91, 101, 113, 119, 124, 127
Cooperatives Hall, 16
cornet, xiv, 18, 24, 26, 29, 30, 59, 63, 64, 68, 69, 70, 77, 80, 85, 86, 93, 94, 99, 113, 114, 115, 124, 128, 129, 130, 144, 146, 147, 152
Cornet Chop Suey, 112
Cornish Will, 54, 66, 67, 70, 71, 74, 153
Cotillion, 19, 20
Cottrell's Hall, 12
Cottrell(e) Louis, 129
Country Dance, 19
Courantes, 2
Cousto(Coustaut)-Desdunes Orchestra, 31
Cousto-Desdunes Orchestra, 28

Creole, xiv, xv, 1, 3, 4, 7, 8, 11, 12, 13, 15, 21, 23, 27, 28, 31, 79, 97, 100, 105, 107, 116, 117, 118, 122, 127, 128, 134, 141, 145, 151, 153
Creoles, 2, 11, 27
Creole Social Clubs, 3
Crescent Jazz Band, 116
cross-rhythms, 102
Cuban and slave music., 3
Cuban Danzon, 103
Cuban or Spanish Orquestas Typicas, 4
Cuban recording, 103
cultural diffusion, 114
cylinder recording of the Bolden Orchestra, 97

Dallas Blues, 116
dance evenings, 15
dance halls, 3, 8, 21, 22, 23, 33, 51, 71, 105, 107, 149
dance music, xiv, xv, 1, 5, 8, 9, 17, 23, 24, 25, 27, 35, 51, 57, 71, 105, 107, 144, 149, 154
dance songs, 51, 52, 54, 145
Dance Songs and Blues, 51
dancing, xiv, 2, 4, 8, 12, 14, 15, 16, 19, 20, 21, 22, 29, 30, 45, 52, 54, 93, 101
dancing to piano or fiddle, 4
Dedroit Johnny, 99
Desdoume Mamie, 60
Desdunes Mamie, 60
discography, 97, 122
ditties, 52
Dixie Queen, 53

Dodds Baby, 19, 21, 47, 59, 86, 88, 92, 134, 152, 156
Doheny John, 103
Doin' the Ping Pong, 54
Don't Go Way Nobody, 40, 41, 82, 130
Dorsey Tommy, 91
Do What Ory Say, 123
Downtown, 2, 11, 12, 13, 16
drums, 24, 32, 113, 115, 126, 148, 155
Dubuclet Laurence, 47
Duhé (Dewey) Laurence, 104
Dunbar Kate, 81
duple time, 33, 45, 48, 79, 91, 155

Eagle Band, 56, 72, 80, 89, 102, 104, 113, 114, 118, 146, 147, 149, 150, 151
early music movement, 98
early music specialists, 76
East Coast Revival, 128
Economy (or Cheapskate) Hall, 12
Economy Hall, 12, 18
Electric Light Hall, 12
Elemental Jazz, xiii, 8, 9, 34, 36, 76, 107, 110, 111, 122, 123, 129, 144
Elemental jazz performances, 111
Elemental Jazz Style, 101, 111
Elemental Style, 114, 125
Emancipation Day, 42, 43
embellishment, 71, 75, 85
embellishments, 125
Ensemble Improvisation, 71, 143, 149
Ernest Giardina's Tonti Social Club Band, 116
European music, 3
European musical tradition, 3

European Revivalist group, 130
extemporise, 110

fake books, 51
Fakers, 80
fakers, 109, 150
Fakers and Readers, 80
Fast Dance Songs, 52
father of white jazz, 6
fiddle, 22
fiddle and caller, 14
Finnerty Paul, 77, 82
First Elemental Jazz Bands, 33
First Generation, 109
first generation of bands, 7, 109
first jazz generation, 104
First St Baptist Church, 61
Fisk Jubilee Singers, 62, 63
five-piece band, 115
Filhé George, 28, 32
folk blues, 91
folk rag, 60
Folk Rag composition, 34
folk ragtime, 34
Folk Songs, 41, 54, 136
folk tune, 57
Fortunea Boo Boo, 108
Foster Pops, 25, 51, 68, 134
Foster Stephen, 43
Fox-trot, 100
fox-trot rhythm, 101
France, 2
Francs Amis, 13
Francs Amis Hall, 32
Frank Christian's Band, 116

Frank Brothers Alcide and Bab Frank, 33
Frank Gilbert "Bab", 89
Fred Keppard's "Dixieland Band", 117
Free Ragtime, 144
free ragtime, 94
French Quarter, 2, 22, 133
French trained musicians, 2
Friendly Societies, 8
friendly societies, 11
Friendly Society dances and Balls, 12
Frog Legs Rag, 48, 49, 94
Funky Butt, 13, 17, 18, 22, 54, 55, 68, 72, 80, 82, 87, 90, 150, 151, 157, 158
Funky Butt Hall, 13, 17, 22, 54, 87
Furniss Paul, 77, 82, 104

Galloway Charlie, 8, 25, 26, 27, 29, 30, 33, 38
Galop, 19
Garden District, 60
Gavottes, 2, 15
Gens de Couleur Libre, 2
Get It Right, 123, 125
Get Out of Here, 52, 53
Get Out of Here (Go on Home), 52
Gettysburg March, 48, 12
Get Your Big Leg Off of Me, 58
Gigues, 2
Glenny Albert, 27, 33, 68, 124
Globe Hall, xiv, 8, 12, 16, 30
Go Down Moses, 61, 62
Golden Rule Band, 104, 109
Golden Rule Orchestra, 89, 113
Gottschalk Louis Moreau, 3

'great man theory' of history, 5
Grizzly Bear, 23
guitar, 24, 25, 27, 28, 29, 30, 55, 56, 68, 69, 84, 87, 88, 92, 113, 115, 117, 128, 146, 148, 155, 156, 158
guitars, 3, 23, 148
Gushee Lawrence, xiv, xv, 1, 8, 23, 26, 27, 28, 29,33, 53, 79, 96, 97, 117, 122, 134
'gut-bucket' or 'tailgate trombone', 115
gutbucket, 21
gut strings, 94, 146
guzzle shops, 22

habanera, 72, 102, 103, 150
Haggert Thornton, 20
Happy Sammy—a Teasin Rag, 54
Happy Schilling's Band, 116
Hardie Daniel, xiii, xiv, xv, 1, 5, 6, 7, 15, 22, 23, 24, 39, 40, 55, 60, 73, 76, 82, 135,146, 152, 158
Harney Ben, 39, 55
head arrangements, 49, 78, 85, 90, 93, 123, 145, 146, 150
heterephony, 72, 149
High Society, 16, 36, 38, 48, 123, 125
Historiography, 122
Holy Roller churches, 4
holy roller hymns, 30
Home Sweet Home, 44, 53, 83
Hopes Hall, 12
Hot Blues, 30
Hot Ragtime, 93
Howe Anthony, 81

Idaho, 44
Ida Sweet as Apple Cider, 44
If the Man in the Moon Were a Coon, 42, 90, 91
If You Don't Like My Potatoes Why Do You Dig So Deep?, 57
If You Don't Shake, 52, 53, 83
If You Don't Shake (You Get No Cake), 52
I May Be Crazy but I Ain't No Fool, 53
Imperial Orchestra, 28, 29, 33, 102, 104, 117
improvisation, 5, 33, 71, 75, 93, 95, 110, 111, 112, 113, 119
Improvise, 110
improvised head arrangement, 104
improvising bands, 15, 20, 71, 94, 149
improvising ensemble, 107
Independence Orchestra, 33,108, 109
individual flourishes, 111
Instrumental Formats, 89
Instrumental Voicing, 85
instrumentation, 36, 71, 76, 78, 99, 105, 116, 119, 120, 122, 124, 126, 128, 130, 146
intricate 'improvised' solos, 106

Jackson Papa Charlie, 61
Jazz, xiii, xiv, xv, 1, 2, 5, 6, 7, 8, 10, 11, 16, 18, 21, 22, 23, 24, 25, 26, 27, 28, 29, 32, 33, 36, 37, 38, 39, 40, 45, 47, 51, 55, 56, 60, 61, 67, 72, 73, 76, 77, 78, 79, 81, 82, 86, 87, 92, 94, 97, 98, 99, 100, 101, 102, 103, 105, 107, 110, 111, 112, 116, 117, 119, 121,

122, 123, 124, 125, 126, 128, 130, 134, 135, 136, 137, 141, 143, 144, 145, 146, 152, 153, 154, 156, 158
jazz, xiii, xiv, xv, 1, 2, 4, 5, 6, 7, 8, 9, 10, 11, 20, 21, 24, 25, 26, 28, 31, 32, 34, 35, 45, 49, 51, 53, 57, 64, 66, 67, 70, 71, 72, 73, 74, 76, 77, 78, 81, 82, 84, 85, 86, 87, 88, 89, 90, 91, 92, 93, 96, 97, 98, 99, 100, 101, 102, 103, 104, 105, 107, 108, 111, 112, 113, 114, 116, 117, 118, 120, 121, 122, 123, 124, 125, 126, 127, 128, 130, 131, 144, 145, 146, 147, 148, 149, 150, 152, 153, 154, 155, 156
Jazz Age, xiii, 125, 145
jazz age sounds of Chicago, 118
jazz historians, 1, 73, 97
Jazzmen, 66, 67, 74, 130, 136
jazz music of the 1920's, 22, 98
jazz revolution, 25
jazz standards, 116, 121, 123, 127
Jeunes Amis, 12, 13
jig, 23, 34, 52
jigs, 3, 5, 14, 23, 35, 154
Johnny Dodds Black Bottom Stompers, 92
Johnny Stein's Band, 116
John Robichaux' Orchestra, 24
John Robichaux's Orchestra, 14, 155
Johnson Bill, 89, 117
Johnson Bunk, xv, 9, 16, 28, 45, 49, 53, 59, 70, 71, 73, 74, 81, 90, 105, 109, 114, 120, 122, 126, 127, 128, 151, 152
Johnson Francis, 5
Johnson Jimmy, 31

Jones Sissieretta, 50, 103
Joplin Scott, 34, 35, 48, 49, 88, 94, 133, 160
jook houses see juke houses
Juba, 23
Jubilees, 4
Jubilee singing, 64
juke houses (jook houses), 14, 25, 56
jump ups, 14, 18, 38, 44, 52, 154
junk man, 31

Katrina (Hurricane), 82
Katz Mark, 87, 108, 112, 135
Kelly Chris, 127
Keppard Fred, 61, 69, 79, 90, 99, 113, 114, 115, 117, 118, 129, 151, 152
Kid Rena's Delta Jazz Ban, 122
King Oliver's band, 16
King Oliver's Creole Jazz Band, 129
Kinney's Hall, 13, 17, 54

Lacoume Emile, 6
Ladies of Providence and the Knights of Pleasure, 18
Laine Jack, 6, 8, 45, 116, 118, 141
La Marseillaise, 45, 141
Lancers, 4, 14, 15
Landau Doug, 121
La Patti Negra, 103
La Praline, 38, 45, 46, 83, 92, 93, 105, 111, 139, 141
La Rocca Nick, 6, 7, 100, 101, 109, 110, 111, 112, 123, 137
Lazy Moon, 38, 44, 92
lead sheet, 80, 93

Les Francs Amis, 11
Lewis Frank, 67, 150
limitations in the early recording methods, 87
Lincoln Park, 68
Little Pussy, 47
local dance hall entertainments, 4
local halls, 8
Lomax Alan, 58, 101, 107, 139
Lomax, John and Alan 58
Longshoreman's (or Jackson's) Hall, 12
Louisiana Purchase, 2
Louis James String Band, 55, 80, 151, 157
Love Charlie, 15, 40, 45, 47, 48, 49
love songs, 113, 124
Low Down Blues, 123, 125
low down blues, 18, 70
Lusitanian Hall, 12
Lusitanos Society, 12
Lyons Bob, 33
Lyttleton Humphrey, 87, 104, 130

Magnolia Band, 115
Make Me a Pallet on the Floor, 18, 57, 59,60, 74, 83, 127
Makin' Runs, 52, 53, 54, 71, 83, 90
Mamie's Blues (2/19 Blues), 57
mandolin, 27, 28, 113
mandolins, 3, 23
Manuel Hall, 29
Manuel Perez, 8, 27, 28, 29, 33, 94, 102, 113
Maple Leaf Rag, 48, 49, 83, 94

March, 16, 18, 33, 39, 48, 49, 64, 66, 73, 92, 93, 123
Marches, 15
Mardi Gras, 2, 18
Marquis Donald, xiii, xiv, 7, 8, 10, 12, 13, 16,17, 18, 21, 22, 26, 29, 30, 55, 56, 58,70, 98, 136, 144
Matson Charles, 129
53, 64, 84, 88, 94
Matthews Bill, 18, 70, 93
Mazooka. See Mazurka
Mazurka, 15, 16, 19, 20, 38, 46, 48, 82, 92, 99, 101, 111, 157, 161
Mazurkas, 14, 15, 21, 47, 92
Melody Based Ensemble Style, 84
melody centred improvisation, 93
melody centred performance, 94
melting pot theory, 5
Mexican bands, 4
Mexican music, 28
Midnight Revellers, 23
military bands, 4
Milneberg Joys, 123, 125
minstrel performances, 94
Minuets, 2
Mississippi River, 40
Mississippi Valley Hall, 12
mixed string and wind orchestras, 4
mixed wind and string ensembles, 9
Moi pas l'aimez ça, 108
Moonwinks, 38, 46, 47, 48, 82, 92, 93, 104
Morton Jelly Roll, 5, 9, 16, 18, 20, 27, 28, 31, 34,45, 46, 53, 54, 55, 59, 60, 61, 68, 80,90, 93, 94, 98, 99, 101,

102, 103, 105,111, 112, 113, 114, 115, 117, 123, 125, 137, 139, 141, 153, 154, 159
Motherless Children, 40
mountain folk song, 58
Mr Johnson Turn Me Loose, 39
Mumford Jefferson 'Brock', 25, 29, 57, 158
musicianers, 110
Muskat Ramble, 57
My Bucket's Got a Hole In It, 56, 127

Napoleon, 2
Ned Louis, 26
neighbourhood dances, 8, 9
New El Dorado, 22
New Orleans, xiii, xiv, 1, 2, 3, 4, 5, 6, 7, 8, 9, 11, 14, 15, 19, 20, 21, 23, 24, 25, 26, 27, 28, 29, 30, 31, 32, 34, 35, 36, 40, 43, 45, 47, 48, 49, 53, 55, 56, 57, 58, 59, 67, 69, 71, 72, 75, 76, 77, 79, 81, 82, 83, 84, 86, 87, 90, 92, 93, 96, 97, 98, 100, 101, 102, 103, 104, 105, 107, 110, 113, 114, 115, 117, 118, 119, 121, 122, 124, 127, 128, 129, 130, 133, 134, 135, 136, 137, 144, 145, 146, 149, 150, 151, 152, 155, 156, 157, 159
New Orleans Blues, 102
New Orleans Diaspora, 127
New Orleans jazz, 102
New Orleans Ragtime Orchestra, 84
New Orleans Revival, 122, 124
New Orleans Style, 97, 122

New Wolverines Jazz Orchestra, 77
Nicholas Wooden Joe, 53, 58, 91, 121, 151
Nobody Knows the Trouble I Have Seen, 43
Noone Jimmy, 126
Northern riff raff, 22
Nunez Alcide, 6

Odd Fellows and Masonic Hall, 12
ODJB. See Original Dixeland Jazz Band
Oh My Darling Clementine, 46
Old Black Joe, 117
Old Brock Cried When The Old Cow Died, 72
Oliver King, 16, 70, 105, 118, 126, 128, 129, 145, 150, 151
Olympia Jazz Band, 81
Olympia Orchestra, 31, 33, 113, 114, 116, 117, 118
One-step, 15, 22
Onward Brass Band, 129
Opera houses, 2
Original Creole Orchestra, xv, 7, 79, 97, 116, 117, 118
Original Dixieland Five, 6
Original Dixieland Jass Band, 6
Original Dixieland Jazz Band, 111, 116
original jazz, 125
Original scores, 38
Orquesta Pablo Valenzuela, 103
Ory Kid, 45, 53, 57, 94, 105, 115, 116, 118, 123, 126, 127, 153
Ory/Oliver Band, 118

Ossman Vess, 80, 92, 104
Over the Waves, 38, 48
Overtures, 15

paddle steamers, 3, 40
Palao Felix, 29
Palao Jimmy, 117
Palm Leaf Rag, 48
Palmer Roy, 88
Panama (W.H. Tyers), 49, 123
Panama Rag (Joplin), 48, 49
Pantages theatre chain, 117
parades, 4, 53
parlour music mode, 93
parlour music of the 19th century, 98
parody dialect, 39
Parody Songs, 39
parody songs, 90
Payne John Howard, 44
Peerless Orchestra, 89, 104, 114, 150
performance practices, 76, 78, 98, 99, 105, 120, 122, 130, 144
performance style, xiv, 30, 71, 147
Perseverence Hall, 12
Petit, Joe 31, 33, 113, 150, 151
Peyton Charles, 20, 29, 33
Peyton's Orchestra, 33
piano, 22, 60, 113
piano 'professors', 8
piano jigs, 35
piano rags, 65, 94
piccolo, 71, 78, 89, 90, 104, 115, 146, 147
piccolo lead, 104
Picou Alphonse, 9, 30, 33, 79, 107, 108, 109, 124, 152, 153

Piron Armand, 33, 86, 113, 114, 116, 118, 129, 150, 151
Piron-Gaspard Dance Orchestra, 113, 114
Piron's New Orleans Orchestra, 129
Piron's Olympia Orchestra, 116
Piron Orchestra, 86, 129
pitch and sonority of the ensemble, 86
plantations, 4, 55
Play Jack Carey, 45, 105
pleasure parks, 9
Polka, 16, 19, 46, 47, 93, 111, 158
Polka Mazurka, 46
Polkas, 15, 21, 38, 92
popular hit tunes, 44
Popular Song and Popular Theatre, 49
Popular Songs, 36, 39
popular songs, 38, 39, 49, 72, 94, 98, 101, 105, 109, 127, 149
popular theatre, 50
popular tunes, 19, 26, 100, 101
Potomac River Jazz Club, 102
pre-arrangement, 112
Pretty Polly, 40
Prince Imperials, 14
protestant churches, 4
proto jazz, 10
Providence Hall, 12, 18, 109

Quadrille, 16, 19, 20, 21, 22, 29, 38, 45, 83, 99, 139, 157, 160
Quadrilles, 4, 14, 15, 19, 21, 113
quadrilles, 17, 19, 20, 28, 154

Raeburn Bruce, 47
rag, xiv, 9, 22, 34, 41, 42, 49, 55, 60, 68, 80, 99
Ragging, 73
ragging, 72, 74, 86, 101, 111, 149, 152
Rags, 35, 36, 41, 42, 48, 49, 59, 83, 86, 90, 91, 102, 111, 127, 135, 158
Ragtime, 15, 16, 33, 35, 38, 46, 57, 72, 74, 84, 88, 93, 102, 113, 115, 117, 133, 135, 144, 145, 149, 151, 154
ragtime, xiv, 4, 9, 14, 16, 28, 33, 34, 35, 39, 42, 48, 49, 52, 53, 54, 55, 60, 67, 73, 74, 79, 84, 86, 88, 91, 92, 93, 94, 99, 100, 101, 102, 103, 105, 111, 112, 113, 116, 117, 119, 120, 123, 145, 151, 153, 158
ragtime era, 112
Ragtime Song, 39
ragtime songs, 4, 39, 42, 88
ratty music, 9
Razzy Dazzy Spasm Band, 6
reading musicians, 109, 110
Reconstruction, 4
recorded jazz, xiii
Red Backed Book of Rags, 49
red light district, 22
reels, 3, 5, 14, 52, 64, 154
refreshments, 17
religious music, 4, 61
Rena Joe, 124
Rena Kid, 122, 123, 124, 125
repertoire, 14, 16, 18, 31, 33, 35, 36, 37, 38, 39, 42, 43, 45, 48, 49, 51, 57, 61, 63, 66, 78, 79, 81, 83, 91, 94, 95, 99, 102, 105, 120, 122, 123, 127, 130, 157, 159, 160
repertoire of traditional jazz, 49
repertory orchestra, 36, 78
revival era, 126
revivalist jazz, 105
revivalist movement, 126
Revivalist music of the 1840's, 4
rhythm section, 84, 85, 88, 89, 99, 113, 115, 126
Ride In Kind Saviour, 63
Ride on King (Jesus), 63, 91
Ride On King Jesus, 61, 64, 83
Ridgeley Bebe, 85, 153
Rippingale Trevor, 77, 81
ritmo de tango, 103
Robert Charles riots, 124
Roberts John Storm, 103
Robichaux John, 14, 15, 24, 28, 34, 45, 104, 155
Robinson Jim, 124
Rose and Souchon, 8, 26
Rouse Don, 102
roustabouts, 40
routineer bands, 100
routineers, 73, 100
Rozelle Orchestra, 88
rumbones, 103
Run Mary (Strumpet) Run, 61
Run Mary Run, 63, 64
Run Nigger Run, 64, 158, 162
Run Sinner Run, 64
Run Strumpet Run, 64
Russel Bill, 47, 72, 74

sacred songs of the white revivalists, 4
saloons, 22
Salty Dog, 57, 61, 152
Sarabandes, 2
Schottische, 15, 38, 48, 92, 157
Schottisches, 4, 15, 21, 92, 113, 156
second decade, 115
second decade of jazz, 111
Sentimental ballads, 43
Sentimental Journey, 92
sentimental songs, 39, 64, 127
Shining Trumpets, 45, 133
Shoo Skeeter Shoo, 39, 42, 43
Shouts, 4
shouts, 30, 57, 61
Silver Leaf Band, 24
Silver Leaf Orchestra, 102
Sissieretta Jones, 50, 103
skiffle music, 26
slap bass style, 113
slave dances, 3
slave music, 3, 51
slaves, 4, 29, 39, 43, 62
slave secular songs and dances, 94
"Slave Songs of the United States", 1867, 63
slide trombone, 24, 104, 105, 108, 113, 115, 116, 124, 126, 128, 145, 153
Slow drag, 16, 72, 160
Smith Charles Edward, 66, 67, 73, 97
Social Dance Evening, 11
social dancing, 93
social halls, 11, 26
Some Of These Days, 116
Song of the Contrabands, 62

sound balance, 87
sounds of early jazz, 76
Southern Rags, 59
Spanier Muggsy, 126
Spanish American musicians, 4
Spanish Guitar., 77
Spanish rhythm, 70, 101
Spanish rhythms, 103
Spanish Tinge Hypothesis, 103
Spasm Band, 27
spasm band, 27
spasm bands, 28
Spirituals, 4, 61, 63, 134
spirituals, 30, 31, 61, 63, 64, 91
split time, 89
spontaneous free improvisation, 111
spontaneous orchestral ragtime, 94
square dances, 19, 20, 33
Stark John, 49
St. Cyr Johnny, 69 91, 92
St. Elizabeth Hall, 12
St. Louis Tickle, 55, 80, 151
stage shows, 44, 50
Stale bread. See Emile Lacoume
Staultz Lorenzo, 55, 56, 102
steel strings, 94, 148
Stewart Dr. Jack, 98, 99, 100, 101, 112, 122, 137, 141
St Nicholas, 22
stock arrangements, 24
stomps, 22
Storyville, 8, 53, 60, 115, 116
Storyville red light district, 8, 115
street band, 27
street bands, 25, 34, 147

street music, 4, 25, 30, 33, 34, 113, 155
street musicians, 34, 35
street music tradition, 4
street performers, 31
street singers, 6, 28
street songs, 25, 30, 31, 38, 99, 105, 119
string band, 24, 26, 28, 29, 108
string bands, 22, 23, 24, 28, 34, 35
string bass, 27, 28, 87, 92, 125
string orchestras, 4
Swanee River, 117
Sweet Adeline, 38, 48, 157
sweet music, 93
swing, 9, 28, 32, 72, 78, 86, 93, 103, 105, 120, 127, 128, 149, 154, 157
Swing Era, 101, 125
Sydney Jazz Club, 81, 82, 101
syncopated cross rhythms, 91
Syncopated dance music, 1
syncopated music, 5, 6, 8, 9, 21, 119
syncopated performance practices, 35
syncopated tunes, 107
syncopated two-beat music, 33
Syncopation, 27
syncopation, 5, 9, 31, 52, 74, 101, 102, 105, 120

tailgate, 45, 105, 113, 115, 125, 145, 147, 153
Texas Tommy, 23
That's Aplenty, 116
Theatres, 2
The Friends Of Hope Society, 12
The Gem, 22
The Holy City, 111

The Old Cow Died and Old Brock Cried, 56, 160
The Tune The Old Cow Died On, 56
Thomson Virgil, 101
Three Step, 46
Three-step mazurka, 46
Tiger Rag, 16, 45, 105, 109, 111, 112, 139, 140, 141
tin band, 23, 24, 29
Tin Band, 24
Tio, 28, 31, 32, 89, 129, 153
Tio-Doublet Orchestra, 31
Tio-Doublet Orchestra, 28
Tirro Frank, 107, 137
Todelo, 23
Tom Brown's Band from Dixieland, 116
transformation, 91, 111, 116, 141
trap drums, 24, 146
trap drum set, 32, 148
tresillo, 103
Très Moutarde, 116
Triple Time, 91
trombone bass runs, 72, 149
Tulane University Jazz Archive, 38
Turkey Trot, 23
Turpin Tom, 48, 159
Tuxedo Cabaret, 115
Tuxedo Orchestra, 89, 104, 115
two-beat style, 79
two-beat vamp based style, 85
two-clarinet formula, 89
Two-step, 14, 15, 16, 17, 19, 28, 33, 34, 38, 72, 113
Two-step dances, 16
Two-steps, 15, 92

Two step, 72

Under the Bamboo Tree, 42, 43, 103
Union Son's Hall, 17
Union Sons Hall, 13, 18
Union Sons Relief Association Hall, 13
Uptown, 2, 4, 8, 12, 15, 20, 21, 29, 38, 107, 154, 158

Valacos Stan, 77, 81, 82
Valentin Boul Boul, 108
valve trombone, 24, 29, 31, 32, 66, 77, 85, 113, 117, 130, 144, 146, 148, 153
vamping bass, 88
Van Der Merwe Peter, 40
'Variating' the Tune, 72
variations, 5, 54, 59, 71, 74, 78, 84, 85, 110, 111, 112, 114, 151
Varieties, 14
vaudeville circuits, 117
vernacular dance songs, 38, 51
vernacular music, 25, 35, 51, 107, 154
Vernacular Songs, 51
Vernacular Style, 91
Viennese Waltz, 48
Vincent Eddie, 117
violas, 23
violin, 24, 28, 68, 69, 71, 72, 78, 80, 81, 84, 85, 86, 87, 89, 90, 93, 99, 103, 104, 113, 114, 115, 116, 126, 127, 129, 130, 144, 146, 148, 149, 150, 151, 155

violinist, 33, 68, 71, 78, 80, 81, 89, 94, 104, 109, 117, 118, 124, 126, 146, 149, 150, 151
violins, 3, 4, 23, 24, 32
virtual reconstruction, 96
Vocal Choruses, 90
vulgar dance songs, 38

W. H. Tyer's *Panama*, 116
Wait till the Sun Shines Nellie, 44, 45
Waltz, 15, 16, 19, 20, 22, 46, 47, 48, 72, 99, 111, 157
Waltzes, 14, 15, 38, 92, 113, 156
waltzes, 4
Washington Post March, 33
Watters Lu, 89, 128
Watzke, Alex (King) 109
wax cylinder recording, 66
Weary Blues, 123
Weltlinger Daniel, 81, 82
Werlein Hall, 12, 13
West Indies Blues, 86, 129, 151
white jazz, xv, 6, 97, 100, 116, 118
white origins theory, 6
Wolverine Orchestra, 128

Yerba Buena Jazz Band, 128

Zacatecas, 54

978-0-595-42555-6
0-595-42555-0